LAMENTATIONS

THE ANCHOR BIBLE is a fresh approach to the world's greatest classic. Its object is to make the Bible accessible to the modern reader; its method is to arrive at the meaning of biblical literature through exact translation and extended exposition, and to reconstruct the ancient setting of the biblical story, as well as the circumstances of its transcription and the characteristics of its transcribers.

THE ANCHOR BIBLE is a project of international and interfaith scope. Protestant, Catholic, and Jewish scholars from many countries contribute individual volumes. The project is not sponsored by any ecclesiastical organization and is not intended to reflect any particular theological doctrine. Prepared under our joint supervision, THE ANCHOR BIBLE is an effort to make available all the significant historical and linguistic knowledge which bears on the interpretation of the biblical record.

THE ANCHOR BIBLE is aimed at the general reader with no special formal training in biblical studies; yet, it is written with the most exacting standards of scholarship, reflecting the highest technical accomplishment.

This project marks the beginning of a new era of co-operation among scholars in biblical research, thus forming a common body of knowledge to be shared by all.

William Foxwell Albright
David Noel Freedman
GENERAL EDITORS

Following the death of senior editor W. F. Albright, The Anchor Bible Editorial Board was established to advise and assist David Noel Freedman in his continuing capacity as general editor. The three members of the Editorial Board are among the contributors to The Anchor Bible. They have been associated with the series for a number of years and are familiar with its methods and objectives. Each is a distinguished authority in his area of specialization, and in concert with the others, will provide counsel and judgment as the series continues.

EDITORIAL BOARD

Frank M. Cross   Old Testament
Raymond E. Brown   New Testament
Jonas C. Greenfield   Apocrypha

THE ANCHOR BIBLE

LAMENTATIONS

INTRODUCTION, TRANSLATION, AND NOTES
BY
DELBERT R. HILLERS

Doubleday & Company, Inc.
Garden City, New York

ISBN: 0-385-00738-8
Library of Congress Catalog Card Number 70–176347
Copyright © 1972 by Doubleday & Company, Inc.
All Rights Reserved
Printed in the United States of America
First Edition
Second Printing

*To the memory
of
my parents*

PREFACE

I have written the following commentary primarily for the general reader, and have included only a limited amount of technical detail. As a result I do not always give explicit credit to the scholar who first proposed a given idea, and, although I cite some differing points of view on controverted issues, I do not always quote the full range of varying opinions. Let it be stated here, then, that I am conscious of my great debt to the many scholars, living and dead, who have occupied themselves with Lamentations, and that I hope my own commentary will attract at least some readers to look further into the extensive and excellent literature on this small book.

To the late William F. Albright, who in his lifetime performed so many acts of kindness and generosity toward me, I am also indebted for the opportunity to work on this interesting segment of the Anchor Bible project. General Editor David Noel Freedman read a draft of the commentary and eliminated many of my blunders and made numerous helpful suggestions. Here and there in the following pages I have expressly acknowledged his contributions, but this does not adequately express the degree to which I am indebted to him. I am grateful also to Mrs. Phyllis Rimbach, who typed the final manuscript. A part of the reading for this commentary was done in the library of the École Biblique in Jerusalem, which hospitably opened its doors to this American visitor as it has to so many others.

CONTENTS

PRINCIPAL ABBREVIATIONS

1. PUBLICATIONS

ANET   *Ancient Near Eastern Texts Relating to the Old Testament*, ed. J. B. Pritchard, 3d ed., Princeton, 1969

BDB   F. Brown, S. R. Driver, and C. A. Briggs, eds., of Wilhelm Gesenius' *Hebrew and English Lexicon of the Old Testament*, 2d ed., Oxford, 1952

BH³   *Biblia hebraica*, ed. Rudolf Kittel, 3d ed., Stuttgart, 1937

BZAW   Beihefte zur Zeitschrift für die alttestamentliche Wissenschaft

CAD   Chicago Assyrian Dictionary

CBQ   Catholic Biblical Quarterly

CTA   *Corpus des tablettes en cunéiformes alphabétiques*, by Andrée Herdner, Paris, 1963

GKC   *Gesenius' Hebrew Grammar*, ed. E. Kautzsch, revised by A. E. Cowley, 2d Eng. ed., Oxford, 1910

JNES   Journal of Near Eastern Studies

JQR   Jewish Quarterly Review

KB³   Ludwig Koehler and Walter Baumgartner, *Lexikon in Veteris Testamenti Libros*, 3d ed., Leiden, 1967

ThR   Theologische Rundschau

UT   *Ugaritic Textbook*, by Cyrus H. Gordon, Rome, 1965

VT   Vetus Testamentum

ZAW   Zeitschrift für die alttestamentliche Wissenschaft

ZS   Zeitschrift für Semitistik und verwandte Gebiete

2. OTHER ABBREVIATIONS

Akk.   Akkadian

Ar.   Arabic

Aram.   Aramaic

Eth.   Ethiopic

Gr.   Greek

Heb.   Hebrew

Phoen. Phoenician
Syr.   Syriac
Ugar.   Ugaritic

H   Hebrew version when chapter and/or verse numbers differ from
        the English
N.F.   Neue Folge
N.S.   New Series; Nova Series

INTRODUCTION

INTRODUCTION

The Meaning and Purpose of Lamentations

"In the fifth month, on the seventh day of the month, in the nineteenth year of King Nebuchadnezzar, king of Babylon, Nebuzaradan, captain of the guard, an official of the king of Babylon, entered Jerusalem. He burned down the house of Yahweh, and the king's house; and all the houses in Jerusalem, including every great man's house, he set on fire and burned. The whole army of the Chaldaeans tore down the walls of Jerusalem, all around. . . . The rest of the people who were left in the city, and those who had deserted to the king of Babylon, and the rest of the populace, Nebuzaradan, captain of the guard, took to Babylon as prisoners. The captain of the guard left only some of the poorest in the country to tend the vines and farm the land" (II Kings 25:8–12).

Thus the book of Kings states the facts about the fall of Jerusalem in 587 B.C. Lamentations supplies the meaning of the facts. It is first of all a recital of the horrors and atrocities that came during the long siege and its aftermath, but beyond the tale of physical sufferings it tells of the spiritual significance of the fall of the city. For the ancient people chosen by Yahweh it meant the destruction of every cherished symbol of their election by God. In line after line the poet recalls all the precious, sacred things which had been lost or shattered: the city itself, once "the perfection of beauty, the joy of the whole earth"; the city walls and towers, once the outward sign that "God is in the midst of her"; the king, "the anointed of Yahweh, the breath of our nostrils"; the priests, and with them all festive and solemn worship; the prophets, and with them all visions and the living word of God; the land itself, Israel's "inheritance" from Yahweh, now turned over to strangers; the people—dead, exiled, or slaves in their own land. Every sign that had once provided assurance and confidence in God was gone.

Thus Lamentations served the survivors of the catastrophe in the first place as an expression of the almost inexpressible horror and grief they felt. Men live on best after calamity, not by utterly repressing their grief and shock, but by facing it, by measuring its dimensions, by finding some form of words to order and articulate their experience. Lamentations is so complete and honest and eloquent an expression of grief that even centuries after the events which inspired it, it is still able to provide those in mute despair with words to speak.

The book is not only an expression of grief, however, but a confession. It is not a perplexed search for the meaning of the catastrophe, still less an attempt to evade responsibility for it. Israel's prophets had foretold with unmistakable clarity the destruction of the nation, and divine punishment for the iniquity of the fathers was the well-known, inescapable darker side of the covenant with God. Lamentations says "Amen" to the prophetic judgment on the sin of the people, and calls it greater than that of Sodom and Gomorrah. Worst of all had been the iniquity of the spiritual leaders. Hence it was Yahweh himself who had consumed Israel. What had come on them was nothing less than the day of the Lord, the day of his wrath.

Central to the book, however, is an expression of hope. It is the merit of Lamentations that it does not quickly or easily promise away the present agony. It does not encourage the remnant of Israel to take comfort in the fathers, or in the exodus, or in the land, or Zion, or the line of David, or any of the old symbols of her status with God. The series of "mighty acts of God" toward Israel had ended with an unmistakable act of judgment, so that the nation's history could be no source of hope. Nor does it at any point forecast a speedy turn in the fortunes of Israel. Instead the book offers, in its central chapter, the example of an unnamed man who has suffered under the hand of God. To sketch this typical sufferer, this "Everyman," the language and ideas of the psalms of individual lament, a tradition quite separate from the national history, are drawn on. From near despair, this man wins through to confidence that God's mercy is not at an end, and that his final, inmost will for man is not suffering. From this beginning of hope the individual turns to call the nation to penitent waiting for God's mercy.

The medium through which these various meanings are expressed is a series of poems composed with deliberate artistry. As is the case with any work of poetic art, so with Lamentations, the meaning is not fully statable apart from the form in which the author clothed it. It cannot be reduced to a set of propositions without serious loss. The present writer offers the above merely as a rough restatement of some major themes in the poems, and prefers to take up more detailed discussion of the meaning of the book only in the COMMENTS which accompany the poems.

THE NAME OF THE BOOK

In the Hebrew Bible Lamentations has the title *'ēkāh,* "How," the initial word of the book. In the Babylonian Talmud, however (Baba Bathra 14b), and in other early Jewish writings, the book is called *qīnōt,* that is, Lamentations. The title in the Greek Bible, *threnoi,* and in the Vulgate, *threni,* is a translation of this Hebrew name. Quite frequently manuscripts and printed editions of the versions will add: "of Jeremiah," or "of Jeremiah the prophet."

PLACE IN THE CANON

The canonicity of Lamentations has never been a matter of dispute. The position of Lamentations in the canon of the Hebrew scriptures, however, is of some importance for the question of authorship. It is never placed among the Prophets, where the book of Jeremiah stands, but is always somewhere in the third division of the Hebrew canon, the Writings (*Ketubim*). Its exact position among the Writings has varied in different ages and in different communities. The Babylonian Talmud (Baba Bathra 14b) records a very old tradition which lists the Writings "chronologically," that is, according to their traditional date; the five Scrolls (*Megillot*) are not grouped together, and Lamentations, which refers to the Babylonian captivity, comes near the end of the list, just before Daniel and Esther. Hebrew bibles, however, reflect liturgical practice in that within the Writings they group the five short books (the "Scrolls," Hebrew *Megillot*) which had come to be read in public worship on five important festivals. The edition commonly used in scholarly study today, Kittel's *Biblia hebraica* (BH³), is based on a manuscript of A.D. 1008 (Codex Leningradensis) which lists the Scrolls in "chronological" order: Ruth, Song of Songs (from when Solomon was young!), Ecclesiastes (from his old age), Lamentations, and Esther. In many manuscripts and printed bibles, however, especially those used by Ashkenazic Jews, the order is that in which the festivals come in the calendar: Song of Songs (Passover); Ruth (Weeks, *Shabuot,* Pentecost), Lamentations (the Ninth of Ab), Ecclesiastes (Tabernacles, Succoth), and Esther (Purim). The second major tradition puts Lamentations just after Jeremiah (Baruch comes between them in some cases). This is the order followed, for example, in the Septuagint (LXX), the ancient Greek translation of the Bible, in the Vulgate, Jerome's Latin translation, and in English Bibles commonly used among Christians. This order was anciently known to Josephus, as may be inferred from his account of the Hebrew canon (*Contra Apionem* I 8), and is also followed by Melito of Sardis (d. 190; see Eusebius *Historia ecclesiastica* IV xxvi 14) and by Origen (Eusebius VI xxv 2). As Jerome explains, this listing fits with an enumeration of the Old Testament books which makes their number agree with the letters of the Hebrew alphabet; "Jeremias cum Cinoth" counts as one book. Jerome, however, does mention the existence of a varying tradition which put Lamentations and Ruth with the Writings ("Prologus Galeatus," *Patrologia Latina* 28, cols. 593–604).

THE DATE OF LAMENTATIONS

The view commonly held by modern scholars agrees closely with the traditional view, that is, that the book of Lamentations was written not long after the fall of Jerusalem in 587 B.C. The memory of the horrors of that event seems to be still fresh in the mind of the author or authors. Moreover, the book at no point testifies to a belief that things would soon change for the better; the kind of hope that appeared in later exilic times had not yet arisen.

Considerable scholarly effort has been expended on determining the order in which the five separate poems were written, but no consensus exists. Wilhelm Rudolph has argued that chapter 1 must date from the first capture of Jerusalem by the Babylonians, that is, from shortly after 597, not from after 587 B.C. His main reason for this view, which has won some adherents, is that chapter 1 does not speak of the *destruction* of the city and temple as do the other chapters, but only of its capture.[1] This is essentially an argument from silence, and is not a secure basis for separating the chapter from the others chronologically. Before Rudolph, other scholars argued for putting chapter 1 somewhat later than 2 and 4. Furthermore, the evidence of the new Babylonian Chronicle shows that the first siege must have been quite short,[2] which does not fit with the references in the chapter to severe famine (1:11, 19; see commentary on 11). Others have wanted to put chapter 3 later than the others because it has a less vivid description of events in the siege than 2 and 4. The truth is that there is insufficient evidence for a precise chronological ordering of the separate laments.[3]

THE AUTHORSHIP OF LAMENTATIONS

That the prophet Jeremiah wrote Lamentations is so firmly rooted in traditions about the Bible, in western literature, and even in art, that even after the ascription to Jeremiah was challenged (first in 1712, by H. von der Hardt[4]), discussion of the book's authorship has tended to take the form of listing reasons why Jeremiah could not have written the book, or why he must have, as though the tradition was unanimous. Ancient tradition on this point is not in fact unanimous, however, and it may clarify the question best if the separate traditions are first listed. Then, as though it were a problem of deciding between textual variants, we may ask: which tradition can best account for the origin of the other?

[1] See Rudolph's commentary on chapter 1 for details.

[2] See Abraham Malamat, "The Last Kings of Judah and the Fall of Jerusalem," *Israel Exploration Journal* 18 (1968), 144–45, for a discussion of the chronology of the events.

[3] The idea that one or more chapters of Lamentations come from the Maccabean period was advanced by S. A. Fries, "Parallele zwischen den Klageliedern Cap. IV, V und der Maccabäerzeit," ZAW 13 (1893), 110–24, but found few adherents. S. T. Lachs, "The Date of Lamentations V," JQR, N.S. 57 (1966–67), 46–56, has revived the idea, but his arguments are equally unconvincing.

[4] Hardt proposed that the five chapters were written respectively by Daniel, Shadrach, Meshach, Abednego, and King Jehoiachin! See Giuseppe Ricciotti, *Le lamentazioni di Geremia* (Turin, Rome, 1924), p. 35. To say that modern critical opinion in this matter was anticipated by Ibn Ezra, as does Lachs, JQR, N.S. 57 (1966–67), 46–47, is erroneous. Ibn Ezra rejects only the rabbinic tradition that Lamentations was the scroll burned by Jeremiah, but not Jeremiah's authorship of the book.

The first tradition does not name any author for the book, and implies that it was not Jeremiah. This is the tradition represented by the Masoretic Text (MT), which says nothing whatever about the authorship of the book, and in which Lamentations is separated from Jeremiah and put among the Writings (*Ketubim*); for details see "Place in the Canon," above.

The second tradition is that Jeremiah wrote the book. The Septuagint prefixes these words to the first chapter: "And it came to pass after Israel had gone into captivity, and Jerusalem was laid waste, that Jeremiah sat weeping and composed this lament over Jerusalem and said —." This heading found in the Greek translation may possibly go back to a Hebrew original, for it is Semitic rather than Greek in style. In the Septuagint Lamentations is placed with other works by Jeremiah. The Vulgate follows the Greek closely, both in the ordering of the book, and in the heading. The Targum (Aramaic translation) ascribes the book to Jeremiah, but in different words and more briefly. It is in accord with other Jewish tradition as recorded, for example, in the Babylonian Talmud (Baba Bathra 15a). In rabbinic writings passages from Lamentations are often introduced by "Jeremiah said." The heading in the Syriac version (Peshitta) titles the work: "The book of Lamentations of Jeremiah the prophet." The oldest of these ancient authorities is the Septuagint.

In spite of the great antiquity of this tradition, it is relatively easy to account for it as secondary to the other. In the first place, there was a very natural desire in the early days of biblical interpretation to determine the authorship of anonymous biblical books. As the one major prophetic figure active in Judah just before and after the fall of Jerusalem, Jeremiah was a candidate sufficiently qualified to meet the demands of a none-too-critical age, especially since certain of his words seemed to fit the theme of Lamentations: "O that my head were waters, and my eyes a fount of tears, that I might weep day and night for the slain of my people" (9:1 [8:23H]). Secondly, there was an explicit statement in the Bible that Jeremiah wrote laments, II Chron 35:25, which is translated here as literally as possible so that some of the difficulties of the verse may stand out: "And Jeremiah sang a lament [or laments] over Josiah. And all the male and female singers spoke of Josiah in their laments, unto this day. And they made them a fixed observance for Israel. And behold they are written in the [book of]

Laments." Actually nothing in the extant book of Lamentations can be taken as referring to the death of Josiah in 609 B.C. The reference to the king in 4:20 must be to Zedekiah, who was king at the fall of Jerusalem. It is difficult to suppose that the Chronicler is simply mistaken, that he actually intended to ascribe authorship of the canonical book to Jeremiah. It is easier to suppose that he gives correct information: Jeremiah, and others as well, composed laments over Josiah, and these were gathered in a book called "Lamentations," but this has nothing to do with the extant biblical book. Nevertheless, the Chronicler's statement that Jeremiah wrote Laments would have encouraged the idea that he was the author of Lamentations, especially since very early on some passages in the biblical book were taken to refer to Josiah (see the Targum on 1:18; 4:20).[5] To sum up, given the anonymous book of Lamentations, it is possible to give a plausible account of how it could have come to be ascribed to Jeremiah, and eventually to be placed after the book of Jeremiah.

If one assumes the opposite, that the book was understood as Jeremiah's from the beginning, it is difficult to suggest any good reason why it was ever separated from his other writings, or circulated without his name. Wiesmann's argument that this was done for liturgical reasons, in order to group Lamentations with the other Scrolls (*Megillot*), is without force, for the oldest listing of the Writings does not group the Scrolls together, and yet includes Lamentations (see above, on "Place in the Canon").

In addition, there is evidence within the book which makes it difficult to suppose that Jeremiah wrote it. Certain statements would be, if not impossible, then at least out of character in the mouth of Jeremiah. For example, 4:17, with its pathetic description of how "we" looked in vain for help from "a nation that does not save," is at variance with Jeremiah's outspoken hostility to reliance on help from other nations (Jer 2:18), and the fact that he did not expect help from Egypt (37:5–10). Would Jeremiah, who prophesied the destruction of the temple, have written 1:10? The high hopes set on Zedekiah in 4:20 ("the breath of our nostrils . . . of whom we said, 'In his shadow we will live among the nations'") are not easy to square with Jeremiah's blunt words to the same king: "You will be given into the hand of the king of Babylon"

---

[5] The idea that Josiah is spoken of in 4:20 was picked up by Saint Jerome and from him by the *Glossa interlinearis,* and thence by later medieval commentators; see Ricciotti, pp. 32–34.

(37:17). "Her prophets find no vision from Yahweh" (2:9) is in the last analysis a rather odd statement from one who prophesied before, during, and after the catastrophe. If 4:19 refers to the flight of Zedekiah (see II Kings 25:4–5) and implies that the author took part, as many suppose (see COMMENT on the passage), then the author was not Jeremiah, who was in prison at the time (Jer 38:28). It may be granted that any of the above-mentioned details has seemed to some scholars compatible with authorship by Jeremiah, and that those who oppose it do not fully agree on which set of arguments proves the case! Even so, these and other details in the book suggest an author or authors more closely identified with the common hopes and fears of the people than it was possible for Jeremiah to be.

Arguments from the language of the book, especially from the vocabulary employed,[6] and from the acrostic form have been used to argue against Jeremianic authorship. These seem indecisive. The lexical evidence seems to suggest that the book has ties with Ezekiel, Second Isaiah, the Psalms, and Jeremiah—that is, its vocabulary not surprisingly resembles that of roughly contemporary writers in some respects.

There is no conclusive evidence as to whether the book is the work of one author, or of several, and both views have been defended in modern times. The unity of form, that is, the fact that all the poems are alphabetic in one way or another, and that the first four have metrical features in common, does suggest that all are the work of one author. One may also point to the fundamental unity in point of view through the whole book, and to resemblances in linguistic detail between one chapter and another. It is possible to read the sequence of chapters as meaningful, which suggests unified authorship or at least intelligent editing. Other scholars, however, find differences in point of view from chapter to chapter (thus 2 and 4 are said to have more of an "eye-witness" character than 1 and 3). The present writer has attempted to interpret the poems as an intelligible unity, whether or not this unity results from one author or from an editor who ordered originally separate works. So as not always to be saying "author or authors,"

[6] The lexical evidence is exhaustively presented in Max Löhr, "Der Sprachgebrauch des Buches der Klagelieder," ZAW 14 (1894), 31–50; cf. "Threni III. und die jeremianische Autorschaft des Buches der Klagelieder," ZAW 24 (1904), 1–16, and "Alphabetische und alphabetisierende Lieder im Alten Testament," ZAW 25 (1905), 173–98, also by Löhr.

the singular form is regularly used in the NOTES and COMMENTS.

Some modern commentators, notably Gottwald, Albrektson, and Kraus, have devoted much effort to delineating the theological traditions on which the author drew, and on this basis have offered conjectures as to the circles from which the book must have come. In Kraus's opinion the author was apparently from among the cult-prophets or the priesthood of Jerusalem, while according to Gottwald he unites the spirit of both priest and prophet, so that the book may offer evidence that there were indeed cult-prophets in ancient Israel.[7] In spite of the value of these minute examinations of the book's theological content, they come close to overemphasizing the individuality of the writer's theology. In actuality the book betrays little one-sidedness, and if it contains themes from various earlier traditions, it seems possible that the author was a layman, and perhaps, as has often been supposed on the basis of 4:19–20, someone connected with the royal court.

PLACE OF COMPOSITION

The events and conditions with which the book of Lamentations deals are without exception located in Judah. Conversely, the book evinces no acquaintance with or special interest in the plight of exiles in Babylon or Egypt. In the absence of any strong evidence to the contrary, then, it seems best to suppose that the book was written in Palestine. Scholars have proposed that the whole book, or parts of it, were composed elsewhere, and it must be conceded that Jews in exile—Ezekiel is a notable example—could be very well informed about conditions back home, but nothing in the book furnishes positive evidence that it was written by an exile.

[7] Gilbert Brunet, in his *Les lamentations contre Jérémie* (Paris, 1968) has recently argued at length that the first four Lamentations were written by a (half-repentant) representative of the nationalist party, probably the high-priest Seraiah, *against* the unpatriotic prophetic party of Jeremiah. The conclusions reached do not agree well with the relatively untendentious character of the book, and are achieved only by a very strained exegesis, a main prop of the argument being that one must distinguish sharply between *ṣar*, "enemy," and *'ōyēb*, "foe," throughout the book. Giorgio Buccellati, "Gli Israeliti di Palestina al tempo dell'esilio," *Bibbia e Oriente* 2 (1960), 199–209, argues from passages in Lamentations that the book comes from a party hostile to Gedaliah: a group of Jerusalemites who opposed his governing from Mizpah, of patriots who hated collaborators. The evidence cited is insufficient to render any of these conclusions probable.

ALPHABETIC ACROSTICS

All five poems in Lamentations are in one way or another shaped according to the Hebrew alphabet. This is most noticeable in the first four poems, which are alphabetic acrostics. Chapters 1 and 2 are of a relatively simple type, in which each stanza has three lines, and only the first word of the first line of each is made to conform to the alphabet, so that stanza one begins with *aleph,* stanza two with *beth,* and so on through the twenty-two letters of the Hebrew alphabet. Chapter 4 is of the same type, but here each stanza has only two lines. Chapter 3 is more elaborate: each stanza has three lines, and all three lines are made to begin with the proper letter, so that there are three lines starting with *aleph,* three with *beth,* and so on. No attempt has been made to reproduce this acrostic feature in the translation given below, for obvious reasons, though the Hebrew letters listed beside the stanzas are intended to call the reader's attention to this phenomenon in the original. Monsignor Ronald Knox did carry through the *tour de force* of reproducing the acrostic in his translation of the Bible, and a sample is quoted here (Lam 4:1–7) to give readers an idea of its effect, though it must be said that Knox strains the English language more than the author of Lamentations did the Hebrew.[8]

> Ah, what straits have I not known, under the
> avenging rod!
> Asked I for light, into deeper shadow the Lord's
> guidance led me;
> Always upon me, none other, falls endlessly the
> blow.
> Broken this frame, under the wrinkled skin, the
> sunk flesh.
> Bitterness of despair fills my prospect,
> walled in on every side;
> Buried in darkness, and, like the dead,
> interminably.
> Closely he fences me in, etc.

Chapter 5 is not an acrostic, but has exactly twenty-two lines and thus conforms to the alphabet to a lesser degree. Other biblical

[8] *The Holy Bible,* trans. Ronald Knox, London, 1955.

poems with twenty-two lines exist—Pss 33, 38, 103—and it is reasonable to suppose that in all these cases the number of lines is chosen intentionally, though none are acrostics.

There are many acrostic poems in the Bible and in other literature, and this commentary is not the place for a full discussion of the form, about which a good deal has been written.[9] Yet it is so prominent a characteristic of Lamentations that some explanation of its purpose and effect must be given. There are really two separate questions involved: the history and purpose of the acrostic form as a whole, and the purpose of the author of Lamentations in using it.

Acrostic compositions were written in both ancient Egypt[10] and ancient Mesopotamia.[11] As is well known, the writing systems of these civilizations were not alphabetic, and therefore their acrostics are not alphabetic either. The most elaborate Mesopotamian acrostic is syllabic. The poem has twenty-seven stanzas of eleven lines each. Each line within an individual stanza begins with the same syllable, and taken together the initial syllables of the stanzas spell out a pious sentence: "I, Saggil-kinam-ubbib, the incantation priest, am adorant of the god and the king."[12] The date of this composition is uncertain, but is probably about 1000 B.C., earlier by far than any datable biblical acrostic. It has been common for scholars to minimize the possibility of a connection between biblical use of acrostics and these extra-biblical works, on the ground that these are syllable or word acrostics as opposed to the alphabetic acrostics inside the Bible, and that they are meaningfully connected with the sense of the poem, as opposed to the meaningless sequence of the letters in the alphabetic type. In spite of these differences, it seems likely that the basic idea of an acrostic, the idea of weaving a pattern of syllables or letters separate from its content into a composition at the beginning or end of the lines, came into Hebrew literature from

[9] Extensive discussions, with bibliography, are offered by P. A. Munch, "Die alphabetische Akrostichie in der jüdischen Psalmendichtung," Zeitschrift der Deutschen Morgenländischen Gesellschaft 90 (1936), 703–10; Ralph Marcus, "Alphabetic Acrostics in the Hellenistic and Roman Periods," JNES 6 (1947), 109–15; Norman K. Gottwald, Studies in the Book of Lamentations, Studies in Biblical Theology, 14 (London, 1962), pp. 23–32.

[10] Adolf Erman, The Ancient Egyptians, trans. A. M. Blackman (New York, 1943), pp. lviii–lix, describes several compositions which, while not acrostic in the strictest sense, have the peculiarity that all the stanzas have the same opening word.

[11] W. G. Lambert, Babylonian Wisdom Literature (Oxford, 1960), p. 67.

[12] Lambert, pp. 63–68.

outside. The major implication is that in discussing biblical acrostics we are apt to be dealing with a phenomenon that is quite ancient and far from its source.

Many explanations for the purpose of acrostics have been suggested, and it is likely that more than one motive was involved. Especially in later times, in medieval magical and speculative works, ideas about the mystical power of the letters of the alphabet seem to have occasioned use of the acrostic form. A more prosaic purpose of acrostics was to aid the memory. Verse is easier to get by heart than prose, and still easier when the sequence of lines follows a set pattern. Finally, acrostics were written for what may be called artistic purposes, to display the author's skill and to make his work a more skillfully wrought offering to his god and to contribute to the structure of the poem. Several writers have proposed that alphabetic acrostics convey the idea of completeness, that is, that "everything from A to Z" has been expressed.[13]

Against this background we may inquire what led the author of Lamentations to use the acrostic form. There is no reason to believe that he or his contemporaries associated magical powers with the alphabet, as was done later. On the other hand, though it is true that acrostic form makes the poems easier to memorize, we have no way of knowing whether this was the author's conscious purpose, or simply an incidental effect. The suggestion that the book was deliberately written as a school exercise (so Munch) is extremely improbable. If the author had any dominating conscious purpose in mind in choosing the acrostic form, it was perhaps to contribute to the artistry of his poems; he thought it made his poems more beautiful. In addition, the acrostic has the effect of controlling and giving form to the poems. It limits and shapes material which is somewhat monotonous and at some points lacking any clear progression of action or thought. Again, it is impossible to be sure that the author consciously intended such an effect.

Those who have expressed an opinion on the artistic worth of these and other acrostic poems in the Bible have generally rated them rather low. Gunkel, for instance, speaks of their composition as "the pious practice of a modest art."[14] Skehan probably speaks

[13] Enno Janssen, *Juda in der Exilszeit*. Forschungen zur Religion und Literatur des Alten and Neuen Testaments 69 (Göttingen, 1956), p. 97; Gottwald, loc. cit.

[14] Hermann Gunkel, *Die Psalmen*, Handkommentar zum Alten Testament, Göttingen, 1926, on Ps 111.

for many in confessing to "being immensely and overwhelmingly bored by Ps. 119,"[15] and others may feel similar ennui at Lamentations. Certainly there is no great intrinsic merit in being able to compose acrostics; as a technical task it cannot have been very difficult. But not all acrostics are of the same merit. In Ps 119 one has the impression that the writer has chosen a large and difficult form which he labors mightily to fill up, like a tax-blank. In Lamentations, the impression is rather of a boundless grief, an overflowing emotion, whose expression benefits from the limits imposed by a confining acrostic form, as from the rather tightly fixed metrical pattern.

A minor peculiarity of the acrostics in chapters 2, 3, and 4 is that two of the letters of the Hebrew alphabet stand in the reverse of their normal order. Usually it is *ayin* before *pe,* and this is the order in chapter 1, but in the other acrostics the sequence is first *pe,* then *ayin.* This peculiarity is found also in the Greek version of Prov 31, and in the opinion of many scholars should be restored in Ps 34, where the conventional order of the alphabet seems to violate the sense. A common explanation, going back to Grotius, is that the order of these letters of the alphabet was not yet fixed at this time. This is sheerly hypothetical, and rather improbable in view of the consistent sequence *ayin-pe* in Ugaritic abecedaries almost a millennium older than Lamentations, and in view of the order of the Greek alphabet, but no more reasonable hypothesis has been advanced. In any case, this variation need not point to different authors for chapter 1 and chapters 2–4.

LITERARY TYPES

Hermann Gunkel carried out an analysis of the five poems in Lamentations which has been very widely followed since. Chapter 5, he wrote, is a communal lament. Chapter 3 is an individual lament in the main, and chapters 1, 2, and 4 are funeral songs—not for individuals, of course, but political or national funeral songs.[16] As Gunkel himself stated, however, all but chapter 5 are mixed,

---

[15] Patrick Skehan, "Wisdom's House," CBQ 29 (1967), 468, note.

[16] "Klagelieder Jeremiae," in *Die Religion in Geschichte und Gegenwart,* 2d ed. (Tübingen, 1929), III, cols. 1049–52. In his discussion of the funeral song, Gunkel draws on the study by Hedwig Jahnow, *Das hebräische Leichenlied im Rahmen der Völkerdichtung,* BZAW 36, Giessen, 1923.

impure specimens of the categories to which they belong: the individual lament in 3 is interrupted by a communal lament (vss. 40–51). The funeral songs contain elements which do not properly belong there, such as the short prayers for help and the invocation of the name of Yahweh. In Gunkel's view, this admixture of alien elements is due to the relatively late date of Lamentations; the book comes from a time when the literary types are no longer kept separate, but are intermingled so thoroughly that even the dominant motif of a particular type may be lost.

Whether this generalization concerning the course of Israel's literary history is valid or not lies outside the scope of this commentary, but it is important to note that we derive relatively little help from form-criticism of the book. If one agrees, for example, that 1, 2, and 4 are funeral songs, one must immediately go on to note the fundamental differences from what is assumed to have been the classic form. Who is supposed to be dead?—the question makes the difficulty evident at once, for the basic situation to which every genuine funeral song is directed is not dominant in these poems. Similarly, in its earlier portion especially chapter 3 may be linked to the psalms of individual lament, but the poem as a whole bursts the confines of this form. Only chapter 5 stays relatively close to the pattern of a traditional literary type. Otherwise, it seems that the writer had no liturgical or literary models which he followed slavishly. On the other hand, in language and imagery he follows tradition rather closely.

SUMERIAN INFLUENCE

The question of Sumerian influence on Lamentations is a separate one. S. N. Kramer, who has edited and translated the principal Sumerian laments over ruined cities, has repeatedly stated that the biblical book of Lamentations is under the direct influence of Sumerian laments. The latest statement of his opinion is as follows: "Just how deeply this mournful literary genre affected the neighboring lands is unknown, no lamentations have as yet been recovered from Hittite, Canaanite and Hurrian sources. But there is little doubt that the biblical *Book of Lamentations* owes no little of its form and content to its Mesopotamian forerunners, and, that the modern orthodox Jew who utters his mournful lament at the 'western wall' of 'Solomon's' long-destroyed Temple, is carrying on a tradition begun in Sumer some 4,000 years ago. . . ."[17] The Assyriologist Gadd is of the same opinion,[18] and such a view has won the adherence of a distinguished commentator on Lamentations, H.-J. Kraus, who writes that the parallels are astounding.[19]

On the opposite side of the question is T. F. McDaniel. Having examined and compared the Sumerian and Akkadian lamentations translated so far, McDaniel concludes that the parallels are not such as to compel one to assume that there was any connection.[20] Such resemblances as do exist can be explained as the result of a common subject matter. Weiser also, in his commentary, finds the resemblances to Sumerian laments very general and unconvincing, and the differences in thought and style much more impressive. He rejects emphatically Kraus's idea that before the fall of Jerusalem there was in Israel a liturgical "Lament over the Ruined Sanctuary."

In the opinion of the present writer, it is difficult to see how the Sumerian texts can have had *direct* influence on the biblical Lamentations. How could an Israelite writer or writers in the sixth century B.C. have had firsthand acquaintance with these Mesopotamian compositions? One must agree that there are genuine, and occasionally close, parallels in wording, but these are to be explained in a wider context. In some cases at least, the literary motifs in the Sumerian laments are paralleled elsewhere in Mesopotamian literature, and where there is a parallel in Lamentations there are parallels elsewhere in the Bible. When we find resemblance between these laments from the early second millennium B.C. and Lamentations, it is most likely evidence of the general truth that in many respects Israel's literature is dependent on an older tradition, and that Mesopotamian literature made a rich contribution to the tradition.

To illustrate the point made above, note the following examples;

[17] S. N. Kramer, "Lamentation over the Destruction of Nippur," *Eretz-Israel* 9 (W. F. Albright Volume, Jerusalem, 1969), 89. Cf. his "Sumerian Literature and the Bible," in *Studia Biblica et Orientalia*, III: *Oriens Antiquus*, Analecta Biblica, 12 (Rome, 1959), p. 201.

[18] C. J. Gadd, "The Second Lamentation for Ur," in *Hebrew and Semitic Studies presented to G. R. Driver* (Oxford, 1963), p. 61.

[19] In the introduction to his commentary, pp. 9–11.

[20] T. F. McDaniel, "The Alleged Sumerian Influence upon Lamentations," VT 18 (1968), 198–209.

the Sumerian texts are quoted in Kramer's translation:[21] "Ur . . . inside it we die of famine // Outside we are killed by the weapons of the Elamites."[22] This is a genuine parallel to Lam 1:20c, and the resemblance is rather striking: "Outside the sword killed my children; inside, it was *famine*" (on the last word, see NOTE). But it is also parallel to Ezek 7:15: "The sword outside, and pestilence and famine inside," and also to Jer 14:18 and Deut 32:25. From a Sumerian text related to the lament genre, the "Curse of Agade" comes a close parallel: "Over your *usga*-place,[23] established for lustrations, // May the 'fox of the ruined mounds,' glide his tail."[24] Compare Lam 5:18 "On mount Zion, which lies desolate, foxes prowl about." But the idea that a ruined city should be the haunt of wild animals is found also in Assyrian royal inscriptions, in an Aramaic treaty (Sefîre I A 32–33) and repeatedly in the Bible. Hence the true situation is that we have to do with a literary convention common to Mesopotamian and biblical literature, and not restricted to the lament genre. A few other Sumerian parallels are quoted in the NOTES below; they are meant to illustrate the persistence of ancient literary motifs into late biblical literature, and not to prove a specific connection of Lamentations to Sumerian laments.

METER, PARALLELISM, SYNTAX, AND STROPHIC STRUCTURE

The acrostic form of the first four chapters permits us in most cases to divide the poems into lines as the author intended. It is partly due to this fortunate circumstance that Lamentations has occupied so prominent a place in the study of Hebrew meter. A more important factor, however, has been the recognition that these lines follow a rhythmic pattern that seems relatively easy to detect and distinguish from other varieties of Hebrew verse. The classic essay on the meter of Lamentations is Karl Budde's "Das hebräische Klagelied" (The Hebrew Song of Lament), which appeared

---

[21] The principal extant Sumerian laments over destroyed cities may be conveniently read in ANET: "The Lamentation over the Destruction of Ur," pp. 455–63; "Lamentation over the Destruction of Sumer and Ur," pp. 611–19; the related "The Curse of Agade," pp. 646–51.

[22] ANET, p. 618, lines 403–4.

[23] The word *usga*, whose proper translation is uncertain, refers to a part of the temple used for lustrations, according to Kramer, ANET, p. 651, n. 70.

[24] ANET, p. 651, lines 254–55.

in 1882 (ZAW 2, pp. 1–52). Although Budde's views still merit restatement, subsequent studies have made important modifications necessary, and in general the unsatisfactory state of our knowledge of Hebrew metrics, a field in which no theory can claim general acceptance, makes it necessary at present to be very cautious in describing the meter of Lamentations.

A brief survey of some competing views may make clear the nature of the difficulty. One major school of thought, the chief representatives being Hölscher,[25] Mowinckel,[26] Horst,[27] and Segert,[28] holds that the decisive characteristic of Hebrew meter (at least in the period we are concerned with) is alternation of stressed and unstressed syllables of the same length, much as in Syriac meter. A more widely followed system has been that of Ley[29] as modified by Sievers[30] and subsequent students. In this system, the basis of Hebrew meter is not syllables, but accents. The various types of lines are distinguished by various numbers and patterns of accents. It is characteristic of followers of this school that rhythmic patterns are symbolized by numbers, thus a line made up of two parts (bicolon), each containing three accents, will be described as 3+3.[31] In recent years a different view has been advocated by David Noel Freedman who describes lines of Hebrew verse according to the number of *syllables* per colon (part of a line) or bicolon, and the rhythmic pattern of syllables within the line, or the number of accents, are not treated as relevant.[32] No full statement of this last theory is yet available, yet it is bound to attract notice if only because older theories encounter great difficulties and have failed to win general acceptance.

With this present uncertainty over the most basic questions in

---

[25] Gustav Hölscher, "Elemente arabischer, syrischer und hebräischer Metrik," BZAW 34 (1920), 93–101.

[26] Sigmund Mowinckel, "Zum Problem der hebräischen Metrik," in *Festschrift für Alfred Bertholet* (Tübingen, 1950), pp. 379–94.

[27] Friedrich Horst, "Die Kennzeichen der hebräischen Poesie," ThR 21 (1953), 97–121.

[28] Stanislav Segert, "Versbau und Sprachbau in der althebräischen Poesie," *Mitteilungen des Instituts für Orientforschung* 15 (1969), 312–21, with references (n. 7) to his earlier studies.

[29] Julius Ley, *Grundzüge des Rhythmus, des Vers- und Strophenbaues in der hebräischen Poesie*, Halle, 1887.

[30] Eduard Sievers, *Metrische Studien*, I–III, Leipzig, 1901, 1904–5, 1907.

[31] Occasionally the same practice is followed in the NOTES and COMMENTS below, without the intention of indicating adherence to the accentual theory.

[32] "Archaic Forms in Early Hebrew Poetry," ZAW 72 (1960), 101–7; "The Structure of Job 3," *Biblica* 49 (1968), 503–8.

mind, we may turn back to Budde's views about Lamentations. According to Budde, the formal unit in Lamentations is a line divided into two parts by a break in sense. The first part of each line is a normal half-line (colon) of Hebrew poetry, while the second part is shorter than the normal colon. This second half-line cannot be only a single word, however, but must be a group of two or more words. Since the first half-line must be at least one word longer, the lines are of the pattern 3+2, 4+3, 4+2, and so on.

Budde found this meter most readily evident in chapter 3, where apparent exceptions are, in his opinion, either indications of textual corruption, or examples of some permissible variants to the normal pattern. For example, occasionally the first colon is shorter than the second, producing a 2+3 line; in such cases one must assume a tension between the artificial poetic rhythm and the actual, natural sentence rhythm. At the cost of somewhat greater effort he goes on to discover the same sort of unbalanced verse in all the lines of chapters 4, 1, and 2, without exception.

Budde went on to assert that this type of verse is found elsewhere in the Bible also, and the evidence suggested that it was the specific meter traditionally used for singing laments over the dead. He therefore titled it *"Qinah"* meter from the Hebrew word for a lament. The potential significance of this theory for the interpretation of Lamentations is obvious, for if it is correct the student of the book is given a very useful tool for reconstructing the text of difficult passages, and also possesses clear evidence connecting Lamentations to the tradition of funeral songs. (There is very general agreement that chapter 5 is in a different rhythm, being divided into cola of equal length, a pattern extremely common in the Old Testament.)

Since Budde wrote, Sievers especially has shown that in Lamentations a sizable proportion of the lines are not in Budde's unbalanced *"Qinah"* meter, but consist of evenly balanced cola.[33] Though scholars would disagree with details of Sievers' own analysis, as he himself anticipated, many would now agree that Budde overstated his case. Some lines are better described as 2+2 (e.g., 4:13a, b) and some are probably 3+3, though there is greater reluctance to recognize the latter type as legitimate, many scholars preferring to emend lines of this sort. Possible examples of 3+3 are 1:1a, 8a, 16a, 21b; 2:9a, 17c, 20a; 3:64, 66; 4:1a, 8b. Thus Budde's view

[33] *Metrische Studien*, I, Erster Teil, 120–23; Zweiter Teil, 550–63.

must be modified by saying that the *"Qinah"* line is at best the dominant line in Lamentations; other metric patterns occur more or less at random throughout the first four chapters. Atypical verses are especially common in chapter 1, and less so in chapter 3. The result of this mixture is that the meter is not nearly as useful in text-criticism as it might be.

A second major modification of Budde's theory is equally important: the dominant verse-type cannot properly be called *"Qinah"* (Lament) meter, because it is used in various classes of Hebrew poems having nothing to do with laments for the dead. Sievers, one of the first to raise this objection, cites as other passages in this meter Isa 1:10–12 (a prophetic oracle of judgment); Isa 40:9 ff. (an oracle of hope); Jonah 2:2–9[3–10H] (psalm of lament by an individual); Song of Songs 1:9–11 (part of a love song), as well as others.[34] Moreover, certain funeral songs are not in *"Qinah"* meter, notably David's lament over Saul and Jonathan (II Sam 1: 17–27). Though scholars have been willing to concede that this "rhythm that always dies away," as Budde called it, seems very appropriate for poetry of a somber character, we cannot use the meter of Lamentations to connect it to a tradition of funeral songs. On the other hand, it is convenient to keep the name *"Qinah"* meter as a handy way of referring to the type.

No attempt has been made in the present translation to reproduce or imitate the meter of the original.[35] Occasionally a line, literally translated, falls into something like the typical *"Qinah"* verse, for example, 3:4:

> He wore out my flesh and skin;
> he broke my bones.

Characterization of the poetic style of Lamentations is not complete without some account of the parallelism found in the poems, and as it turns out this raises further questions concerning the meter.

---

[34] *Metrische Studien*, I, Erster Teil, 116.

[35] Such an undertaking lies beyond my powers; when I attempt metrical translation I achieve something like the following by Vavasour Powell, *Sippor Ba-Pach*, or *The Bird in the Cage* (London, 1662), p. 143:

> How doth the city sit alone
> that full of people was?
> How is she become a widow?
> she that was great alas!

Quoted in Rolf P. Lessenich, *Dichtungsgeschmack und althebräische Bibelpoesie im 18. Jahrhundert*, Anglistische Studien, 4 (Cologne, Graz, 1967), p. 11.

Poetic parallelism may be illustrated by almost any verse from chapter 5 of Lamentations, for example, 5:2:

> Our land is turned over to strangers;
> Our houses, to foreigners.

The second colon corresponds to and resembles the first, that is, there is a semantic association between "land" and "houses" and between "strangers" and "foreigners," and in this case the verb of the first colon is to be understood also with the second though it is not repeated. Such resemblance between poetic units is, as is well known, a pervasive feature of Hebrew poetry, and is found to some extent throughout Lamentations. But parallelism is not present in *all* the lines of Lamentations. (By line I mean a line of Hebrew text as printed in Kittel's *Biblia hebraica*[3], which is a satisfactory working definition.) Disregarding what has traditionally been called "synthetic" parallelism, that is, cases where a line may be separated into two parts but where there is no clear semantic or grammatical resemblance between the two,[36] 104 out of the 266 lines in the book do not exhibit parallelism (39 per cent). More significant is the contrast between chapter 5 and the first four chapters. There is a much higher proportion of parallelism in 5, where only three lines out of twenty-two (14 per cent) do not have parallelism. One may note that two of these lines, 5:9 and 10, while without internal parallelism, might be regarded as parallel to each other (external parallelism). By contrast, in the first four chapters 101 of 244 lines (41 per cent) do not contain parallelism. This contrast amplifies our notion of the different poetic style employed in chapters 1–4 as over against 5, which is not solely a metrical difference.

Even though others would undoubtedly disagree with the present writer concerning the presence or absence of parallelism in individual verses, the general pattern sketched above may probably be regarded as correct. If so, our description of the meter is affected. We have described it above as consisting of *"Qinah"* verse for the most part, that is lines having a longer first colon, followed by a shorter second colon. Interspersed, it was said, are lines consisting of equal parts. When parallelism is obviously present, there is no difficulty with this description; for example, in 2:7: "Yahweh rejected his own altar; he spurned his sanctuary," there is no problem in deciding what are the cola, and where the division

---

[36] If it were desired, one could restate the results in terms of the proportion of synonymous to synthetic parallelism, without change.

between them lies. But when parallelism is not present, the question of where to divide the verse becomes acute. Or is it correct to assume that the verse is divided at all? Budde, and others after him, speak of a division produced by a "break in sense," but this is vague, and in practice it seems that Budde and others have followed a kind of intuition as to where the caesura comes, rather than any rigorously defined principle. Lines without parallelism consist for the most part of a single sentence, thus, for example, 1:2b: *'ēn lāh mᵉnaḥēm mikkol 'ōhᵃbehā* (word for word: "There-is-not to-her a-comforter out-of-all her-lovers"). To make two parts out of these lines with only one sentence, it is necessary to divide at a great variety of places with respect to syntax: between nominal subject and verb in 1:1c; between a prepositional phrase modifying a verb and a following nominal subject, in 1:1b; between a nominal subject and a prepositional phrase modifying it, in 1:2b; between verb and prepositional phrase modifying it, in 1:3c—and so on through almost every combination of sentence elements. To put it in another way, it seems impossible to define syntactically where the division between cola (caesura) is to be made in these lines. At least no one has yet offered a satisfactory definition.[37] If one is to continue to describe these lines as made up of two cola, then probably it will be necessary to argue that the dominant pattern set up by the lines with parallelism shapes our reading of these lines. Otherwise one may prefer to describe the lines without parallelism as undivided.

Several further observations concerning the poetic style of Lamentations arise from studying the syntax of the verbal sentences in the book. In a study so far published only in part,[38] Francis I. Andersen has analyzed all the verbal sentences in Genesis which

---

[37] J. Begrich asserts that the caesura cannot interrupt a construct chain, or fall between the two accented syllables in a word with two accents; obviously these restrictions still leave a great deal of room open. See his "Der Satzstil im Fünfer," ZS 9 (1933–34), 173.

[38] The writer regrets the necessity of referring to the conclusions of a work not easily available to readers, and which Professor Andersen would doubtless revise and amplify in some respects before publication. There is, however, no similar work available for comparison. I have taken the liberty of altering Andersen's technical terminology in some respects in favor of terms which, while less precise, are more traditional and hence apt to be more readily intelligible without lengthy explanation. For verbless clauses, the reader is referred to Andersen's monograph *The Hebrew Verbless Clause in the Pentateuch*, New York, Nashville, 1970. For a fuller discussion, see the writer's contribution to the forthcoming Festschrift for J. M. Myers.

have more than one modifier following the verb. By modifier is meant any element such as direct object, indirect object, adverb, prepositional phrase functioning as an adverb, etc. The subject of the verb is also classified as a modifier, and studied in relation to the other post-verbal elements. On the basis of over a thousand sentences of this sort, Andersen is able to present an abstract theoretical model of the verbal sentence, showing the relative order of the modifiers with respect to each other. As it turns out, there is a great regularity in this respect, and only about 4 per cent of the examples diverge from the normal order. This study of prose usage provides an extremely useful basis for comparison with Lamentations. The results obtained by applying the same methods of analysis to the verbal sentences in Lamentations show that a much higher proportion of sentences with two post-verbal modifiers display abnormal order, about 26 per cent (32 of 122 sentences). Most of the abnormal examples in Lamentations involve the position of a nominal subject or a nominal direct object with respect to a prepositional phrase. In this sort of sentence the "abnormal" order is nearly as common as the "normal." In sentences with three post-verbal modifiers the contrast is still more marked. According to Andersen's study 64, or about 15 per cent of the 409 examples in Genesis, were aberrant, differing from the normal pattern. Of twenty-seven such sentences in Lamentations, nineteen, or 70 per cent, do not follow the pattern most common in Genesis.

It is reasonable to propose as a hypothesis that metrical or rhythmic considerations have dictated this divergence from normal prose order where it takes place. Somewhat surprisingly, this is not obviously true, at least not from the point of view of an accentual system of meter, or as far as "*Qinah*" meter is concerned. In 2:20c, for example, *'im yēhārēg bᵉmiqdaš 'ᵃdōnāy kōhēn wᵉnābī'* (word-for-word: Are-slain in-the-sanctuary of-the-Lord priest and-prophet?), the order is prepositional phrase = subject, abnormal as compared to what is most common in Genesis. Yet the opposite order would seem to be possible here from the point of view of meter. Variant orders appear within the space of a single colon; compare 1:20b *nehpak libbī bᵉqirbī* (word-for-word: Is-turned-over my-heart inside-me) to 2:9a *ṭābᵉ'ū bā'āreṣ šᵉ'ārehā* ("have-sunk into-the-earth her-gates"). Until further refinement of our metrical conceptions or of our knowledge of Hebrew syntax is achieved, the proper conclusion seems to be that in the ordering of these sentence-elements the poet of Lamentations was freer than the writers of Genesis, and his choice of a particular order was dictated by what may vaguely be called "stylistic" considerations, rather than meter. Whether this is a characteristic of other Hebrew poetry is as yet undetermined.

One rhythmic consideration does seem to have played a part, however. In sentences with three post-verbal modifiers, the poet shows a marked tendency to put the *longest* element last, regardless of its normal relative order. For example, in 2:6b it is syntactically unusual for the prepositional phrase to precede the nominal direct object:

šikkaḥ yahweh beṣiyyōn   mōʿēd wešabbāt

("has-made-forgotten Yahweh in-Zion   festival and-sabbath").

But the compound direct object is very long as compared to the other modifiers in the sentence. Andersen noticed a similar tendency in sentences in Genesis where word order was unusual, so that this may be a rather widespread characteristic of Hebrew sentence rhythm. On the other hand, it is present in such a high proportion of sentences in Lamentations that it may deserve notice as a feature of poetic style.

The acrostic pattern in chapters 1–4 quite obviously divides these poems into units which may for convenience be called strophes, or stanzas. In some cases these strophes correspond to units of thought. Thus, for example, 1:2 presents a unified picture— Zion weeps by night, forsaken by all her friends—quite clearly separated from what goes before and follows after. In other cases, however, the pattern marked off by the acrostic does not coincide with the pattern of thought. Ideas and images may be run-on from one acrostic unit to the next. The last line of the *Daleth* strophe is 3:12, but the image of God as an archer is continued into the first line of the *He* strophe, 3:13. This syncopation seems particularly common in chapter 3; see COMMENT there.

NOTE ON A FEATURE OF POETIC DICTION

Phrases of the pattern "daughter (Heb. *bat*) X," or "virgin daughter (*betūlat bat*) X" occur twenty times in Lamentations, a remarkable number in so short a book, since such phrases occur only about forty-five times in all the rest of the Old Testament. Jeremiah has sixteen of these other occurrences, including eight occurrences of *bat 'ammī* (lit., "daughter of my people"), practically the only occurrence of the term outside Lamentations (the exception is Isa 22:4). It is reasonable to conclude that this poetic device was especially popular in the seventh and sixth centuries B.C., although it was no doubt very ancient, since Micah and Isaiah use it.

Lamentations uses *bat ṣiyyōn*, "Zion," seven times; *bᵉtūlat bat ṣiyyōn*, once; *bat 'ammī*, "my people," five times; *bat yᵉhūdāh*, "Judah," twice; *bᵉtūlat bat yᵉhūdāh*, once (these last two are not used elsewhere in the Bible); *bat yᵉrūšālaim*, "Jerusalem," twice, and *bat 'ᵉdōm*, "Edom," once.

These phrases serve a poetic purpose in two ways. First, they help make explicit the personification of the people or city as a woman. Secondly, they seem to serve metrical purposes. The longer forms, the ones with three elements such as "virgin daughter Zion" are used to stretch out a name so as to make a whole poetic unit (colon) out of it. The shorter, two-part, phrases such as "daughter Zion" seem also to serve metrical purposes, though these are not clearly definable given the present state of understanding of Hebrew metrics. The most easily observable pattern is that phrases of the type "daughter X" tend to stand last in the unit of parallelism (colon). This is true of all occurrences in the Bible with a few exceptions (Jer 4:31; 6:26; 8:21; 51:33; Ps 137:8). There are practically no exceptions to this rule in Lamentations, the only possible case (4:3) being open to question textually (see NOTE).

As has been observed by others, the renderings familiar from older English translations, and the Revised Standard Version (RSV), "Daughter *of* Zion," "virgin daughter *of* Zion," etc., are potentially misleading, since the Hebrew phrases refer to the people or city as a whole, and not to a part of it. To put it another way, the relation between the two nouns in such a phrase is one of apposition; the second is not the possessor of the first. Since the main purpose of "daughter" and "virgin daughter" seems to be metrical, they have in most cases been omitted in the present translation. Where this has been done it is mentioned in the NOTES. This omission seemed advisable especially since no thoroughly idiomatic English is available. The new Jewish Publication Society (JPS)

version uses "Fair Zion," "Fair Maiden Judah," "my poor people,"
and the like, which seem fairly close to the effect of the Hebrew.

The Text

The Hebrew text of Lamentations is in a relatively good state of
preservation, compared to the text of some other biblical books.
This advantage in the commentator's favor is to some extent balanced by a corresponding disadvantage: the ancient translations
offer relatively little help at those places where the Masoretic text,
that is, the received Hebrew text, may be suspected of being
corrupt. At the end of a recent thorough study of the text, Bertil
Albrektson concludes that the Septuagint, the ancient Greek translation, was based on a text in all essentials identical with the
Masoretic text, and the same verdict is offered for the Syriac
version.[39] It is now believed that the Greek text of Lamentations
belongs to the recently identified *kaige* recension,[40] that is to say,
the Greek text in our possession is the outcome of a deliberate
attempt to accommodate the original Greek translation as closely
as possible to a near forerunner of the Masoretic text. Thus the
Greek also gives us for the most part a text that already contained
the errors and difficulties that are in the standard Hebrew text. Under these circumstances, commentators are compelled to rely to a
greater degree on conjectural emendation of corrupt passages than
might otherwise be necessary.

Among the Dead Sea scrolls published so far, in addition to
small portions of the canonical book Lamentations, are several

[39] Bertil Albrektson, *Studies in the Text and Theology of the Book of
Lamentations*, Studia Theologica Lundensia, 21 (Lund, 1963), pp. 208–13.
The other most important recent treatment of the text is Wilhelm Rudolph,
"Der Text der Klagelieder," ZAW 56 (1938), 101–22.

[40] Jean-Dominique Barthélemy, *Les devanciers d'Aquila*, Vetus Testamentum
Supplements 10 (Leiden, 1963), pp. 33, 138–60, is quite positive about the
identification of the Greek text of Ruth, the Song of Songs, and Lamentations
as belonging to the *kaige* group, and bases a theory about the beginning
of liturgical use of these books on the identification. Frank M. Cross, Jr.,
"The History of the Biblical Text in the Light of Discoveries in the Judaean
Desert," *Harvard Theological Review* 57 (1964), 283, is somewhat more
reserved: "Ruth and Lamentations are good candidates" (to be representatives
of the recension). See also J. M. Grindel, "Another Characteristic of the
Kaige Recension: *nṣḥ/nikos*," CBQ 31 (1969), 499–513; note that LXX has
nikos for *nṣḥ* at Lam 3:18 and 5:20.

fragments of a poetical composition which incorporates many quotations from Lamentations, often in paraphrased form (4Q179).[41] This composition is occasionally cited in the NOTES as an early interpretation of the sense of the text.

LITURGICAL USE

The poems in Lamentations may have been used in public mourning over the destruction of Jerusalem immediately after they were written, though the evidence is inconclusive. Nothing in the poems precludes such a use. Formal characteristics, such as the use of "I" in many passages, do not rule out the use in corporate worship, nor does the use of acrostic form compel us to think that chapters 1–4 were intended only for private study and devotion (so Segert). On the other hand, the alternation among various speakers in some of the poems does not justify the conclusion that they were acted out publicly as a ritual drama. Nor is there evidence for the existence of a fixed liturgical practice of "Lament over the Ruined Sanctuary" already in pre-exilic times (against Kraus; see above under LITERARY TYPES). Direct evidence for liturgical use of Lamentations is not available until the Christian era.

Public mourning over the destroyed city was carried on from earliest times. Jer 41:5, narrating an event just after the death of Gedaliah, the governor installed over Judah by the Chaldaeans, tells of "eighty men from Shechem, Shiloh, and Samaria who had shaved off their beards, torn their garments, and lacerated their skin," coming to make offering at the house of Yahweh in Jerusalem. Zech 7:3–5, dated to 518 B.C., hence shortly after the return from exile, makes it clear that mourning and fasting in the fifth month (Ab) had been going on ever since the city fell. Zech 8:19 also refers to a fast in the fifth month. It is, therefore, reasonable to suppose that the Lamentations were used in connection with this regular public mourning already in the exilic period.

[41] J. M. Allegro, with Arnold A. Anderson, *Qumrân Cave 4*, Discoveries in the Judaean Desert of Jordan, V (Oxford, 1968), pp. 75–77; cf. J. Strugnell, "Notes en marge du volume V des 'Discoveries in the Judaean Desert of Jordan,'" *Revue de Qumrân* 7, No. 26 (1970), 250–52.

Presumably continuing this ancient practice, later Jewish usage assigns Lamentations a place in the public mourning on the 9th of *Ab,* the fifth month, which falls in July or August according to the modern calendar. The 9th is chosen in preference to strict adherence to either of the two biblical dates (II Kings 25:8–9 gives the 7th of *Ab;* Jer 52:12 gives the 10th) because of the tradition that the *second* temple fell to Titus on the 9th of *Ab,* and that Bar Kokhba's fortress Betar fell on that date in A.D. 135.

In various Christian liturgies portions of Lamentations are used in services on Maundy Thursday, Good Friday, and Holy Saturday, a custom which has resulted in the composition of eloquent musical settings of the text.

In modern times, Leonard Bernstein has used texts from Lamentations in his "Jeremiah" Symphony (1942), for mezzo-soprano and orchestra, as did Igor Stravinsky, in his "Threni" (1958), for solo voices, chorus, and orchestra.

SELECTED BIBLIOGRAPHY

Much fuller listing of works on Lamentations will be found in the commentaries of Kraus, Rudolph, and Wiesmann; the last-named is especially valuable for its extensive listing of medieval works. When an author's name is cited in this commentary without the name of his work, the reference is to the work listed here.

COMMENTARIES AND SIMILAR WORKS

Albrektson, Bertil. *Studies in the Text and Theology of the Book of Lamentations.* Studia Theologica Lundensia, 21. Lund, 1963.

Budde, Karl. "Die Klagelieder," in *Die fünf Megilloth.* Kurzer Hand-Commentar zum Alten Testament. Freiburg i. B., Leipzig, and Tübingen, 1898.

Ehrlich, Arnold B. *Randglossen zur hebräischen Bibel,* VII. Leipzig, 1914.

Ewald, Heinrich. *Die Dichter des alten Bundes.* Vol. I, 2: *Die Psalmen und die Klagelieder,* 3d ed. Göttingen, 1866.

Gelin, Albert. *Jérémie—Les Lamentations—Le Livre de Baruch.* La Sainte Bible de Jérusalem. Paris, 1951.

Gordis, Robert. "A Commentary on the Text of Lamentations," in *The Seventy-Fifth Anniversary Volume of the Jewish Quarterly Review,* eds. Abraham A. Neuman and Solomon Zeitlin, pp. 267–86. Philadelphia, 1967.

———— "Commentary on the Text of Lamentations (Part Two)," JQR, N.S. 58 (1967–68), 14–33.

Gottwald, Norman K. *Studies in the Book of Lamentations,* Studies in Biblical Theology, No. 14. Rev. ed. London, 1962.

Haller, Max. *Die Klagelieder: Die fünf Megilloth.* Handbuch zum Alten Testament. Tübingen, 1940.

Keil, Carl Friedrich. *Der Prophet Jeremia und die Klagelieder.* Biblischer Commentar über das Alte Testament, eds. C. F. Keil and Franz Delitzsch. Leipzig, 1872.

Kraus, Hans-Joachim. *Klagelieder* (Threni). Biblischer Kommentar. 3d ed. Neukirchen-Vluyn, 1968.

Löhr, Max. *Die Klagelieder.* Die Heilige Schrift des Alten Testaments. 4th ed., edited by Alfred Bertholet. Tübingen, 1923.

———— *Die Klagelieder des Jeremia.* Handkommentar zum Alten Testament. Göttingen, 1893.

———— *Die Klagelieder des Jeremias.* Göttingen, 1891.

Meek, Theophile J., and W. P. Merrill. *The Book of Lamentations.* The Interpreter's Bible, vol. VI, 1–38. New York and Nashville, 1956.

Oettli, Samuel. "Die Klagelieder," in *Kurzgefaszter Kommentar zu den heiligen Schriften Alten und Neuen Testaments,* eds. Hermann Strack and Otto Zöckler, pp. 199–224. A: Altes Testament, 7. Abteilung: Die poetischen Hagiographen. Nördlingen, 1889.

Paffrath, Tharsicius. *Die Klagelieder.* Die Heilige Schrift des Alten Testaments, eds. Franz Feldmann and Heinrich Herkenne, vol. VII, 3. Bonn, 1932.

Plöger, Otto. *Die Klagelieder.* Handbuch zum Alten Testament. Erste Reihe, 18. 2d ed. Tübingen, 1969.

Ricciotti, Giuseppe. *Le lamentazione di Geremia.* Turin, Rome, 1924.

Rudolph, Wilhelm. *Das Buch Ruth—Das Hohe Lied—Die Klagelieder.* Kommentar zum Alten Testament, vol. XVII, 1–3. Gütersloh, 1962.

Weiser, Artur. *Klagelieder.* Das Alte Testament Deutsch, 16, pp. 297–370. Göttingen, 1962.

Wiesmann, Hermann. *Die Klagelieder.* Frankfurt am Main, 1954.

ARTICLES AND MONOGRAPHS

Ackroyd, Peter R. *Exile and Restoration: A Study of Hebrew Thought of the Sixth Century B.C.* Philadelphia, 1968.

Beer, Georg. "Klagelieder 5,9," ZAW 15 (1895), 285.

Begrich, Joachim. "Der Satzstil im Fünfer," ZS 9 (1933–34), 169–209.

———— "Zur hebräischen Metrik," ThR 4 (1932), 67–89.

Boehmer, Julius. "Ein alphabetisch-akrostichisches Rätsel und ein Versuch es zu lösen," ZAW 28 (1908), 53–57.

Brunet, Gilbert. *Les lamentations contre Jérémie: Réinterprétation des quatre premières lamentations.* Bibliothèque de L'École des Hautes Études, Section des Sciences Religieuses, vol. LXXV. Paris, 1968.

Buccellati, Giorgio. "Gli Israeliti di Palestina al tempo dell'esilio," *Bibbia e Oriente* 2 (1960), 199–209.

———— "In Lam. 2,5," *Bibbia e Oriente* 3 (1961), 37.

Budde, Karl. "Das hebräische Klagelied," ZAW 2 (1882), 1–52.

Cannon, William Walter. "The authorship of Lamentations," *Bibliotheca Sacra* 81 (Dallas, 1924), 42–58.

Caro, Hermann Isaak. *Beiträge zur ältesten Exegese des Buches Threni mit besonderer Berücksichtigung des Midrasch und Targum.* Berlin, 1893.

Driver, G. R. "Hebrew Notes on 'Song of Songs' and 'Lamentations,'" in *Festschrift für Alfred Bertholet,* eds. Walter Baumgartner et al., pp. 134–46. Tübingen, 1950.

———— "Notes on the Text of Lamentations," ZAW 52 (1934), 308–9.

Emerton, J. A. "The Meaning of *'abnē qōdeš* in Lamentations 4:1," ZAW 79 (1967), 233–36.

The Five Megilloth and Jonah. Introductions by H. L. Ginsberg. The Jewish Publication Society of America. Philadelphia, 1969.

Fries, S. A. "Parallele zwischen den Klageliedern Cap. IV, V und der Maccabäerzeit," ZAW 13 (1893), 110–24.

Gelin, Albert. "Lamentations (Livre des)," *Dictionnaire de la Bible. Supplément,* vol. 5, cols. 237–51. Paris, 1957.

Gunkel, Hermann. "Klagelieder Jeremiae," in *Die Religion in Geschichte und Gegenwart.* 2d ed. Vol. III, cols. 1049–52. Tübingen, 1929.

Hölscher, Gustav. "Elemente arabischer, syrischer und hebräischer Metrik," BZAW 34 (1920), 93–101.

Horst, Friedrich. "Die Kennzeichen der hebräischen Poesie," ThR 21 (1953), 97–121.

Jahnow, Hedwig. *Das hebräische Leichenlied im Rahmen der Völkerdichtung.* BZAW 36. Giessen, 1923.

Janssen, Enno. *Juda in der Exilszeit.* Forschungen zur Religion und Literatur des Alten und Neuen Testaments 69 (N.F. 51). Göttingen, 1956.

Joseph, Max. "Tisch'a Beaw," in *Jüdisches Lexikon,* vol. IV/2. Berlin, 1930.

Kraus, Hans-Joachim. "Klagelieder Jeremiä," in *Die Religion in Geschichte und Gegenwart.* 3d ed. Vol. III, cols. 1627–29. Tübingen, 1959.

Lachs, Samuel Tobias. "The Date of Lamentations V," JQR, N.S. 57 (1966–67), 46–56.

Ley, Julius. *Grundzüge des Rhythmus, des Vers- und Strophenbaues in der hebräischen Poesie.* Halle, 1887.

Löhr, Max. "Alphabetische und alphabetisierende Lieder im Alten Testament," ZAW 25 (1905), 173–98.

———— "Sind Thr. IV und V makkabäisch?" ZAW 14 (1894), 51–59.

———— "Der Sprachgebrauch des Buches der Klagelieder," ZAW 14 (1894), 31–50.

———— "Threni III. und die jeremianische Autorschaft des Buches der Klagelieder," ZAW 24 (1904), 1–16.

Lohfink, Norbert. "Enthielten die im Alten Testament bezeugten Klageriten eine Phase des Schweigens?" VT 12 (1962), 260–77.

McDaniel, Thomas F. "The Alleged Sumerian Influence upon Lamentations," VT 18 (1968), 198–209.

———— "Philological Studies in Lamentations, I–II," *Biblica* 49 (1968), 27–53, 199–220.

Malamat, Abraham. "The Last Kings of Judah and the Fall of Jerusalem," *Israel Exploration Journal* 18 (1968), 137–55.

Marcus, Ralph. "Alphabetic Acrostics in the Hellenistic and Roman Periods," JNES 6 (1947), 109–15.

Meinhold, Johannes. "Threni 2,13," ZAW 15 (1895), 286.

Mowinckel, Sigmund. "Zum Problem der hebräischen Metrik," in *Festschrift für Alfred Bertholet,* eds. Walter Baumgartner et al., pp. 379–94. Tübingen, 1950.

Munch, P. A. "Die alphabetische Akrostichie in der jüdischen Psalmendichtung," *Zeitschrift der Deutschen Morgenländischen Gesellschaft* 90 (1936), 703–10.

Perles, Felix. *Analekten zur Textkritik des Alten Testaments.* Neue Folge. Leipzig, 1922.

Porteous, Norman W. "Jerusalem—Zion: The Growth of a Symbol," in *Verbannung und Heimkehr* (Rudolph Festschrift), ed. Arnulf Kuschke, pp. 235–52. Tübingen, 1961.

Praetorius, Franz. "Threni I, 12. 14. II, 6. 13.," ZAW 15 (1895), 143–46.

Robinson, Theodore H. "Anacrusis in Hebrew Poetry," in *Werden und Wesen des Alten Testaments.* BZAW 66 (1936), 37–40.

———— "Notes on the Text of Lamentations," ZAW 51 (1933), 255–59.

———— "Once More on the Text of Lamentations," ZAW 52 (1934), 309–10.

Rudolph, Wilhelm. "Der Text der Klagelieder," ZAW 56 (1938), 101–22.

Segert, Stanislav. "Versbau und Sprachbau in der althebräischen Poesie," *Mitteilungen des Instituts für Orientforschung* 15 (1969), 312–21.

———— "Zur literarischen Form und Funktion der fünf Megilloth (Im margine der neuesten Kommentare)," *Archiv Orientální* 33 (1965), 451–62.

Sievers, Eduard. *Metrische Studien* I–III. Leipzig, 1901, 1904–5, 1907.

Westermann, Claus. "Struktur und Geschichte der Klage im Alten Testament," ZAW 66 (1954), 44–80.

Wiesmann, Hermann. "Der planmäszige Aufbau der Klagelieder des Jeremias," *Biblica* 7 (1926), 146–61.

—— "Die Textgestalt des 5. Kapitels der Klagelieder," *Biblica* 8 (1927), 339–47.

—— "Der Verfasser des Büchleins der Klagelieder ein Augenzeuge der behandelten Ereignisse?" *Biblica* 17 (1936), 71–84.

—— "Der Zweck der Klagelieder des Jeremias," *Biblica* 7 (1926), 412–28.

Zenner, P. J. K. "Thr 5," *Biblische Zeitschrift,* o.s. 2 (1904), 370–72.

LAMENTATIONS

I
"Is there any pain like my pain?"
(1:1–22)

Aleph	1 How deserted lies the city that once was full of people! Once greatest among nations, she is now like a widow; Once the noblest of states, she is set to forced labor.
Beth	2 By night she weeps aloud, tears on her cheeks. There is no one to comfort her of all her lovers. All her friends have betrayed her, have become her enemies.
Gimel	3 Judah has gone into exile after suffering and after much toil. She dwelt among the nations but found no rest. All who pursued her cornered her in narrow straits.
Daleth	4 The roads to Zion mourn, since none come in for the feasts. All her gates are desolate. Her priests sigh, Her virgins are troubled, and she is bitter.
He	5 Her enemies came out on top; her foes have it easy, For Yahweh afflicted her for her many rebellions. Her children were driven as prisoners before the enemy.

Waw   6 And there has departed from Zion all her
        splendor.
      Her princes were like stags which could
        find no pasture,
      But went on exhausted before the hunter.

Zayin   7 Jerusalem calls to mind the days when
        she was banished in misery,

    . . . .

      When her people fell into the enemy's
        grasp and there was no one to help.
      Her enemies saw her and laughed at her
        collapse.

Heth   8 Because Jerusalem sinned so great a sin,
        people shake their heads at her.
      All who once respected her, despise her,
        having seen her naked.
      She herself groans aloud, and falls back
        frustrated.

Teth   9 Her pollution has fouled her skirts. She did not
        think of the consequences for her.
      And she has come down astonishingly, with
        no one to comfort her.
    "Yahweh, look upon my misery, at the
        insolence of the enemy!"

Yod   10 The enemy stretched out his hand after all her
        precious things.
      She saw that the heathen entered her
        sanctuary,
      Concerning whom you had commanded:
      "They shall not enter your assembly."

Kaph   11 All her people are groaning, seeking food.
      They gave their darlings for food, to keep
        alive.
    "Yahweh, look and consider how worthless I
        have become!

Lamed   12 Come, all you who pass by on the road, consider
        and see:

Is there any pain like my pain—that
which he caused me,
Which Yahweh inflicted on me on the
day of his burning anger?

Mem 13 From on high he sent fire and sank it into my
bones.
He stretched a net for my feet; he turned
me back.
He made me desolate, sick all day long.

Nun 14 Watch is kept over my steps. They are
entangled by his hand.
His yoke is on my neck. He has brought
my strength low.
The Lord has given me up to those
whom I am powerless to resist.

Samekh 15 The Lord heaped up in my midst all my
strong men,
Then summoned an assembly against me
to crush my young warriors.
The Lord trod the wine-press of fair
young Judah.

Ayin 16 Over these things I weep; my eyes run with
water.
For any comforter, anyone to console, is
far from me.
My children are desolate because the enemy
has prevailed."

Pe 17 Zion spread out her hands — there was none to
comfort her.
Yahweh commanded Jacob's enemies to
gather around him.
Jerusalem has become like an unclean
thing in their midst.

Sade 18 "Yahweh is in the right, for I disobeyed his
command.
Listen, all you peoples, and realize my
pain!

My young men and women have been
taken prisoner.

Qof   19 I called for my lovers, but they deceived me.
My priests and my elders expired in the
city
While seeking food to keep alive.

Resh   20 Yahweh, see how I am in anguish! My bowels
churn.
My heart is turned over inside me, when I
think how rebellious I was.
Outside the sword killed my children;
inside, it was famine.

Shin   21 Listen to how I groan! There is no one to
comfort me.
All my enemies heard of my trouble; they
rejoiced that you had done it.
Oh bring on the day you proclaimed, and
let them be like me!

Taw   22 Let all their wickedness come before you, and
do to them
Just what you did to me for all my
rebellions.
For many are my groans, and my heart
is sick."

Before 1:1 of MT, the LXX has this preface: "And it came to pass after Israel had been taken captive and Jerusalem had been laid waste, Jeremiah sat weeping and lamented this lament over Jerusalem, and said —" The Vulgate also contains this prologue, in nearly identical form. Though this is a later addition to the text, based on the identification of Jeremiah as author of the book, note that the style is Hebraic rather than Greek. Either it was translated from a Hebrew *Vorlage,* or the author imitated the style of biblical Greek.

1:1. . . . *once was full of people!* For a line of strikingly similar construction and thought-pattern, contrasting a glorious past with the wretched present, cf. Isa 1:21: "How she has become a whore, the faithful city!" On *rabbātī ʿām* as "full of people," cf. I Sam 2:5 *rabbat bānīm,* "having many sons." These parallels seem to make the traditional understanding preferable to the otherwise attractive suggestion of T. McDaniel, *Biblica* 49 (1968), 29–31, that in view of the Phoenician and Ugaritic divine title *rbt* one should render *rabbātī* in the first and second lines as: "The Mistress of the people . . . the Mistress among the nations." This destroys the contrast with *bādād* in the first half-line; moreover, the extra-biblical parallels are not exact.

The epithets in lines 1b and 1c consist of a noun modified by another noun with the preposition *b,* and hence contrast with the construct chain of line 1a (*rabbātī ʿām*). The question is: what is meant by this *b?* It could mean "over" or "among." (Rudolph renders the first as "among" [*unter*] and the second "over" [*Fürstin über die Gaue*], but it seems better to attempt to render it the same in both lines, in view of the very close parallelism.) A translation "over" has often been preferred, especially for *śārātī bammᵉdīnōt*, "princess over provinces"; this is then often taken to refer to provinces ruled from Jerusalem in the days of Josiah. But one may question whether *śārātī bammᵉdīnōt* would be idiomatic Hebrew for "princess *over* provinces." The masculine title *śar* (the feminine is of infrequent occurrence) regularly stands in construct before the thing ruled; note, e.g., *śārē hammᵉdīnōt*, I Kings 20:14, 15, 17, 19; Esther 8:9; 9:3. (Exceptions are only apparent; in Ps 45:16[17H], *b* after *śārīm* is distributive, local: "princes *throughout* the whole land"; similarly I Chron 12:21[22H], *śārīm baṣṣābā'* is "officers *in* the army," not "over the [whole] army".) In favor of "among," note that expressions like "great among (*b*) nations" are good Hebrew equivalents for the superlative. Note such use of *b* in Jer 49:15; Prov 30:30 and other examples cited in BDB, s.v. *b*, § 2a. Note that a Qumran composition incorporating citations from Lamentations, 4Q179, Fragment 2, line 5, paraphrases with *śrty kl l'wm̊[ym]*. If translated as is done here, lines 1b and 1c imply that the poet is not limiting the picture strictly to the "city," but has the whole state in mind; elsewhere also the poem occasionally has a wider perspective in view, note "Judah" in vs. 3; "Jacob" in vs. 17.

The sequence *rbty . . . śrty* in this verse is tantalizingly similar to a pair of Ugaritic adjectives, the standard epithets following names of cities, e.g., *'udm* (a city-name) *rbt* // *'udm ṯrrt* (the first adjective means "great"; meaning of the second is uncertain). One may perhaps think of a reinterpretation within Hebrew poetic tradition of a pair of words that had become partly obscure over the centuries. Note that Heb. *rabbāh* follows the proper names of cities in *ṣīdōn rabbāh*, Josh 11:8, and *ḥᵃmat rabbah*, Amos 6:2.

2. A detail in 2a illustrates how late biblical poetry retained but modified age-old poetic tradition. The verbs *bākāh*, "weep," and *dāmaʿ*, "shed tears," are commonly used parallel to one another already in Ugaritic poetry, *bākāh* always in the first half-line (or colon, to use more convenient terminology). That is to say, in the useful terms introduced by M. Held, *bākāh* is A-word to *dāmaʿ* as B-word (cf. Jer 13:17). Here also the verb *bākāh* is used first, quite in the old style, but instead of a parallel verb there is a verbless sentence with the noun *dimʿāh*, "tears," as subject.

3. Though some versions and commentators have taken *min*, "from," here as causal, "on account of" (cf. Isa 5:13 *gālāh ʿammī mibbᵉlī daʿat*) this is very strained in the present case, and involves

the necessity of taking *gālāh* in a sense, "to migrate (voluntarily)," which it does not really have, in spite of Ezek 12:3 and II Sam 15:19, which are often cited for this sense. Hence the preposition must be taken as "out of." The idea is that the actual catastrophe came after a long period of inglorious trouble and toil. Moreover, as Rudolph has argued with special persuasiveness, the remainder of the verse also refers to Judah's troubles *before* the captivity. "She dwelt among the nations" means "she was once an independent nation among the nations of the earth." Many commentators have thought otherwise, and indeed the line by itself could also refer to the scattering of the Jews "among the nations" following the fall of Jerusalem, which is often mentioned in the Old Testament, and in Lam 2:9 also ("among the heathen"). Since the combination of the verb *yāšab*, "to dwell," with "among the nations" does not occur elsewhere, it is especially difficult to decide between the two interpretations, but the view that this is a reference to pre-exilic conditions seems preferable as being more in harmony with the whole chapter, which is not otherwise concerned with the plight of the exiles among the heathen. Note the close parallel to the sentiment of 4:20: "In his shadow we will *live among the nations*," an unambiguous reference to the pre-exilic period of independent nationhood.

cornered her in narrow straits. Literally "overtook her between the narrow places." Since the Hebrew phrase *bēn hammᵉṣārīm* is un-paralleled, the exact sense is uncertain. A "Thanksgiving Psalm" from Qumran (Hodayoth [1QH v 29]) paraphrases this line and adds "so I could not get away."

4. To *šōmēmīn*, with plural in *-īn*, cf. *tannīn* 4:3. The odd form *nūgōt* is probably best explained as a Niphal participle of *yāgāh;* so most commentators, cf. G. Bergsträsser, *Hebräische Grammatik*, II. Teil (Leipzig, 1929), para. 26g. LXX's "led away," even if genuine and not due to inner-Greek corruption (so Albrektson), is not a good parallel to "sigh" in the first colon; note, however, Nahum 2:8[7H]. To 4a compare "Lamentation over the Destruction of Sumer and Ur," ANET, p. 612, line 39: "That no one tread the highways, that no one seek out the roads." This is part of a curse pronounced by Utu (line 26). Cf. also Isa 33:8; Judg 5:6.

5. *have it easy*. The correctness of MT *šālū* is demonstrated (against Ehrlich) by use of this verb in a similar context in Jer 12:1.

6. "And" at the beginning of this verse is rather awkward, since the connection to the preceding line is not very close, and since in

good Hebrew poetic style one does not begin new lines with "and," to say nothing of new stanzas. In the present case, this is an artificiality into which the author was led by the acrostic. Since there are practically no other words in Hebrew beginning with *w,* the sixth letter of the alphabet, he must use the conjunction *w* ("and") here and in 2:6; 3:16–18; 4:6. Aside from these six occurrences, where choice of the verb-form has been dictated by the acrostic, the writer of Lamentations uses *waw*-consecutive with the imperfect twenty-three times. This kind of form is not characteristic of archaic Hebrew poetic style, but the quantity of such forms in Lamentations is a sufficient indication that style had changed in this respect by the sixth century B.C. (Note that with no real exceptions the LXX supports the MT with respect to *waw*-consecutives.) *Waw*-consecutive forms tend to occur in just two poetic situations, a characteristic not easily reflected in translation. Of the twenty-three, seven occur at the beginning of the final line of a three-line stanza (1:6c; 2:3c, 5c, 6c, 8c, 14c, 17c) and one (4:11b) at the head of the final line of a two-line stanza. The other characteristic use is in a line such as 2:15b, where two verbs occur in the first colon in the line, and the second is a *waw*-consecutive form. This style of line is most common as the middle line of three (five times: 2:15b, 16b; 3:2, 5, 11) and occurs just once as the first of three lines (3:43), and once as the third line (3:12). Outside of these two characteristic uses, *waw*-consecutive forms are decidedly unusual. Anomalous occurrences in 1:9b, 13a, and 2:4b may point to textual problems. 3:37 is a special case, the *waw*-consecutive being in what amounts to a quotation (see the NOTE there). This leaves four cases (1:8c; 3:33, 53; 4:11) which are real exceptions to the general pattern. Since a pattern exists, one may ask what effect was intended. Where the *waw*-consecutive stands first in the final line of a stanza, it seems reasonable to suppose that the verb was meant to mark and emphasize the end of the strophe. The effect of the second characteristic use is discussed in the NOTE at 3:2.

Zion. Heb. "Daughter Zion."

7. In the MT and the ancient versions there are four lines. After line 1 (7a) comes "All the precious things she had in olden times" (if this line, 7b, is included, the Hebrew of 7a would be translated in a slightly different way: "Jerusalem calls to mind, during the days when she was banished in misery," etc). Since the rigid stanza form rules out a four-line stanza in this chapter (as also in 2:19),

most commentators have preferred to leave out MT's 7b as inter-
rupting the thought sequence, in preference to omitting 7c or 7d (7a
must be kept for the acrostic), and that has been done here. Recently
Rudolph and Albrektson, following Ehrlich, argue for eliminating
the line beginning "When her people" (7c). They argue that to say
"Jerusalem calls to mind the days," as one must if 7b is omitted,
would mean that those days are in the past—which is not the case,
as shown by the rest of the poem. However, "the days" seems to
be explained by 7c, "When her people fell into the enemy's grasp,"
as a reference to the actual days of the fall of the city and the beginning of the exile, a period which was in the past from the writer's
point of view. Since acceptable sense is obtained, in fact, whether 7b
or 7c is omitted, it is perhaps best to conclude with Meek that this
strophe circulated in two different text-forms with identical first and
third lines, the extant text being a conflation of the two. There seems
little decisive reason for preferring either reading as the original.

   when she was banished in misery. Heb. *m⁽ᵉ⁾rūdehā* is rare and
of uncertain meaning. It seems to form a hendiadys with *'onyāh,*
to judge from similar juxtapositions at 3:19 and Isa 58:7 (if the
text of these passages is in order), and is so translated here. The
Greek renders *m⁽ᵉ⁾rūdehā* with *apōsmos,* "repulsion, driving away."

   fell into the enemy's grasp. In this context, where not only death
but also exile is in the picture, this translation for Heb. *binpōl
'ammāh b⁽ᵉ⁾yad ṣār* seems preferable to "Fell *by* the enemy's hand."
The latter translation is possible, but is not the only acceptable
rendering of the Hebrew phrase (contra Ehrlich, followed by Meek):
note especially II Sam 24:14.

   collapse. Heb. *mišbattehā* is a *hapax legomenon,* often emended by
commentators, but since it may well be related to *šābat,* "to stop,
cease," and the sense thus obtained fits the context well, MT is best
retained.

   8. *people shake their heads at her.* Literally, "For that reason
she has become a *nīdāh.*" Heb. *nīdāh* occurs only here. Ibn Ezra,
and in modern times Löhr and Rudolph, take this as "object of
head-nodding," i.e., "object of scorn," comparing Hiphil *hēnīd
b⁽ᵉ⁾rō'š,* "shake the head"; cf., e.g., Jer 18:16; Ps 44:15[14H].
This has been followed here (so also Gordis). Noteworthy also is
the explanation in LXX and in the famous medieval Jewish commentator Rashi, where *nīdāh* is connected with *nūd,* "to wander"; on
the abstract noun for a person or body of persons, cf. *gōlāh* and

gālūt. Either of these explanations seems preferable to changing the text to *niddāh,* "unclean, i.e., menstruating, woman"; even though this reading is reflected in Aquila, Symmachus, and the Syriac, and is favored by many moderns, it seems to be a case of substitution of a well-known, hence easier, word, for a rare one.

aloud. Heb. *gam* is ordinarily "also, too," but this is inappropriate here. A homonym *gm,* "aloud" or the like, occurs often in Ugaritic with the verb *ṣḥ,* "to cry out," and has been identified with some plausibility in a number of biblical passages. McDaniel first suggested that *gam* means "aloud" in this passage, see *Biblica* 49 (1968), 31–32, with references to other notes on the subject.

9. The text of 9b seems rather short, since there are only two words, and accents, in the first colon. The use of *waw*-consecutive is also unusual compared to the general pattern in Lamentations (see NOTE on vs. 6). One might suppose, then, that a verb has been lost at the beginning of the line, and that *wattēred* was originally the second verb in the kind of coordinate construction common in the book. It would be hazardous to restore the missing word, but it may have something like "She has fallen."

10. The last two lines, especially the third, are cases where the second colon in the line is longer than the first, if the Hebrew text is divided as the syntax seems to suggest.

12. MT *lō' 'ᵃlēkem,* lit. "no/not to you," is generally conceded to be corrupt in some way, although some have defended it. Ancient Jewish tradition (see Caro) took the *lō' 'ᵃlēkem* as "may it not come upon you" and some moderns have explained the text so, but this is forced. Of various efforts to emend the text, the conjecture *lᵉkū,* "come," proposed by F. Praetorius, ZAW 15 (1895), 143, has the merit of being simple, and of bearing some resemblance to the existing text, and has been followed here as probably approximately correct. To the sequence "Come . . ." followed by a question beginning with *'im,* one may compare Isa 1:18: "Come . . . if your sins are as scarlet," etc.

Which he caused me. Heb. *'ōlal* is a passive verb as pointed in the MT, but since "Yahweh" is explicitly mentioned as the subject of an active verb in the next line, it seems preferable to suppose that this is one of the cases where the text has been very slight retouched to avoid ascribing to Yahweh the responsibility for pain or the like. See the NOTE on 4:16 below. "Yahweh" is the subject of *'ōlēl* in vs. 22.

13. *sank it.* Read *yōrīdennāh,* reversing the order of *w* and *y* at the beginning of MT *wayyirdennāh.* LXX, which is very consistent otherwise in rendering Hebrew *waw*-consecutive by *kai,* does not have *kai* here and supports the proposed reading. The reading of MT breaks the line at an unsatisfactory place and the implied verb *rādāh,* "to rule," yields no satisfactory sense. Note that *yārad,* "to come down," is used of fire from God, as proposed here, in II Kings 1:10, 12, 14; II Chron 7:1. Use of an imperfect for past time, after a perfect in the first half-line, is unusual, and not paralleled exactly anywhere else in Lamentations, but occasionally one does find a rather similar sequence of forms (cf. 1:14a; 2:22; 4:1–2), so this is perhaps not an insuperable objection to the emendation.

14. The translation of 14a is based on retaining the consonants of MT, but (a) reading *nisqad* (with some Hebrew manuscripts) for *nisqad. nisqad* is a *hapax legomenon,* which may have arisen after other parts of the line had been misunderstood; *nisqad* would be the Niphal (not otherwise attested) of *sqd,* a well-known verb regularly followed by *'al,* as here. The verb is used in a hostile sense here, as in Jer 5:6; 44:27; Dan 9:14. (b) Reading not *pᵉšā'ay,* "my sins," which does not fit as subject of "are entangled," *yiśtārᵉgū,* in the following clause, but rather *pᵉšā'ay,* "my steps," a rare word found in I Sam 20:3 and perhaps to be restored in Prov 29:6; a related verbal form occurs in Isa 27:4. (Perles already suggested *pᵉšā'ay,* but treated the rest of the clause differently.) *śarag* is used only one other time in biblical Hebrew, and hence biblical evidence alone is not likely to indicate adequately the range of meaning and usage of the verb. In defense of the meaning proposed here, note that in the Aramaic of the Babylonian Talmud the cognate verb is used (in Ithpeel) of entangling the foot in a chain; see Marcus Jastrow, *Hebrew-Aramaic-English Dictionary* (New York, 1950), s.v. *kablā'* and *srag.* In Syriac *srag* is used of a path: *'urḥā dabtuqlātā srīgā (h)wāt,* "a road beset *or* entangled with stumbling blocks," cited from R. Payne Smith, *Compendious Syriac Dictionary* (Oxford, 1903), s.v. *srag.* For the idea expressed, see the COMMENT. This rendering may at least claim to respect the consonantal text, and is perhaps defensible linguistically, but is, of course, far from certain. Praetorius proposed in ZAW 15 (1895), 143–44: "The yoke of my sins *is heavy,*" *niqšāh 'ōl pᵉšā'ay,* and has been followed by others, including recently Kraus. Already the Targum translated

nisqad as "was heavy." Rudolph modifies Praetorius' suggestion: "My sins weigh heavy on me," *niqšū ʿalay pᵉšāʿay*.

His yoke. Read *ʿullō*, with Symmachus, for MT *ʿālū*, "they have gone up." MT has perhaps been influenced by the plural ending of the preceding verb. A plural verb does not fit with the singular verb later in the line: "He/it brought low." Possibly, however, the original text has been partially lost through haplography, and we should read *ʿālāh ʿullō ʿal*, etc., "His yoke has gone up on," etc. Cf. the NOTE on 5:5 below. Rudolph, following Budde, favors a similar solution.

The syntax of 14c is somewhat unusual, but MT is retained here on the supposition that the clause following *bīdē* is a relative clause without relative pronoun, following a noun in construct (so Rudolph and others).

The Lord. *ʾᵃdōnāy* occurs fourteen times in Lamentations: *yhwh*, "Yahweh," the proper name of God, occurs thirty-two times. Outside of the isolated *ʾēl*, "God," at 3:41 and *ʿelyōn*, "Most High," in 3:35, 38, these are the only divine names in the book. Rather strikingly, *ʾᵉlōhīm*, "God," does not occur at all. The variation between *ʾᵃdōnāy* and *yhwh* seems to be haphazard. There is no convincing explanation for it from the point of view of meaning, for in a given passage one seems about as appropriate as the other. Also metrically there is no apparent ground for preference of one over the other. Finally, one may note that there is considerable variation between the two in the manuscript tradition. It seems impossible to be sure that the usage was absolutely uniform even in the original form of the book, even though it is likely that to some extent *ʾᵃdōnāy* has replaced an original *yhwh*, especially since in later periods *ʾᵃdōnāy* was being pronounced, in public reading, wherever *yhwh* stood in the text. The practice in the present translation is to follow the reading given by Codex Leningradensis, the manuscript printed in Kittel's *Biblia hebraica*, in the absence of any certain criterion for determining the original reading in a given verse.

15. The verb *sillāh* with which the verse begins is difficult. It is often rendered "despised" or "flouted" (RSV) as if from a rare verb *slh* "to despise" (elsewhere only at Ps 119:118 and there in Qal, not Piel), but this does not fit well with the following "in my midst," which seems to demand a verb describing a physical action. The translation "heaped up" is based on seeing here a root *slh* (*sly*) equal in sense to the well-attested *sll*, "to heap up." (Alternately,

one might suppose that *sillāh* is a scribal error for a form of *sll*.) *sll* is used in Jer 50:26 of heaping up sheaves of grain ("sheaves" is a widely accepted correction, involving metathesis of two consonants, for an otherwise unintelligible word) preparatory to threshing; this is in turn a picture of the punishment to be inflicted on Babylon. Note that the Targum here has *kᵉnas*, "gathered." If it is correct to translate "heap up" here, the imagery of the verse is consistent, harvest metaphors being used throughout (see the COMMENT). The Syriac renders *sillāh* by *kbaš*, "he trampled down"; the etymology which the translator had in mind is not clear.

16. *my eyes.* MT has *'ēnī 'ēnī*, "my eye, my eye," a clear case of dittography, i.e., of copying one word twice by mistake. Read simply *'ēnī*, with LXX, Syriac, and Vulgate. M. Dahood, *Rivista Biblica . . . Italiana* 8 (1960), 364–65 (not available to me, cited in McDaniel, *Biblica* 49 [1968], 32–33) has proposed reading *'ēn 'ēnī*, "the fount of my eyes," deleting the suffix from the first noun and comparing Ugar. *qr 'nk*, "the fountain of your eyes." One may doubt, however, that such a construction, consisting of a noun meant in one of its senses in construct before a form of the same noun meant in another sense, existed in biblical Hebrew. Note that a more normal meter, with the second colon shorter than the first, is obtained by deleting one *'enī* as a dittography. (The Targum cleverly renders MT by "my two eyes!")

desolate. Heb. *šōmēmīm* is an adjective usually used of cities, less often of people as here (so II Sam 13:20; Isa 54:1).

17. The *b* in *bᵉyādehā* is instrumental (lit. "with her hands") cf. Josh 8:18.

unclean. I.e., menstruous, and hence ceremonially impure. Parallels to this metaphoric use are found in Isa 30:22; 64:5[6H]; Ezek 7:19–20; Ezra 9:11.

18. The appeal to "all nations" to hear is relatively rare; a fairly close parallel is Ps 49:2[1H]; cf. I Kings 22:28; Micah 1:2.

19. McDaniel has argued, in *Biblica* 49 (1968), 33–34, that *hēmmāh* here should be taken as the Hebrew counterpart of Ugar. *hm*, "behold," and it must be conceded that "they" is slightly out of place in this line, where no emphasis on the pronominal subject is intended. But vs. 8 (*hī'*) and possibly vs. 21 (*'attāh*) seem to provide parallel examples where an independent pronoun is used as verbal subject for no obvious reason as far as sense is concerned, so that one suspects that metrical considerations have dictated the use

of the pronoun, an explanation which would cover the present case
also.

On the meaning of "lovers" cf. COMMENT on vs. 2.

The rest of this verse is somewhat difficult, and hence the text
translated here is possibly not correct. The second line is short, being
2+2 according to the principle of counting accents, and therefore
some suggest that a word has been lost. Note, however, that there
are other relatively short lines in this chapter (2b, 4c, 8c, 13c), so
that this line is perhaps not impossible as it stands. In structure it is
very similar to 18c, as pointed out to me by D. N. Freedman. In
the third line (19c), LXX and Syriac add: "and they did not find
(any)." Some commentators (recently Kraus) have accepted this
as the original second half of the line, and delete MT "to keep alive,"
which is syntactically somewhat difficult. But it seems more likely that
"and they did not find (any)" is an explanatory addition to the difficult MT (so Albrektson). The MT is kept here, then, especially
since the syntax: perfect verb followed by imperfect verb with the
conjunction *waw*, expressing purpose, is not totally unparalleled; see
BDB, s.v. *w*, who compare II Kings 19:25; Isa 25:9.

20. *My heart is turned over*, etc. Cf. Hosea 11:8. JPS translates
"I know how wrong I was to disobey" comparing Exod 14:5.

Famine. Read *kāpān* (cf. Job 5:22; 30:3 and Aram. *kapnā'*) for
MT *kammāwet*, "like death," which it seems to me cannot be made
to yield satisfactory sense despite repeated efforts by interpreters to
defend it. Or perhaps read **kapnūt*, cf. Syr. *kapnūtā;* though unattested in Hebrew, the form with abstract termination would better
explain the development of MT. [The asterisk designates a hypothetical reconstruction—a word presumed to exist, but nowhere in-
stanced in any text.] The present conjecture is based especially
on Ezek 7:15: "The sword outside, and pestilence and famine
inside; he who is in the field shall die by the sword, and he
who is in the city—famine and pestilence shall devour him"; and Jer
14:18: "If I go out to the field, there are those slain by the sword,
and if I go into the city, there are the diseases of famine." Cf. also
Deut 32:25, and from the "Lamentation over the Destruction of
Sumer and Ur," ANET, p. 618, lines 403–4: "Ur . . . inside it we
die of famine // Outside we are killed by the weapons of the Elamites."

21. *Listen*. Based on repointing as imperative instead of the perfect ("they heard") of MT, which may have arisen under the in-

fluence of the perfect *šāmᵉ'ū* of the next line. In view of the other singular imperatives or precatives addressed to God in the immediate context, a singular imperative, which would imply that Yahweh is addressed (so the Syriac), is preferable to a plural, which would be addressed to other men or peoples (so the Greek, cf. vs. 18).

The second line of this verse (21b) is much the longest line in the chapter. Commentators have favored dropping various words or phrases. Possibly the line is a conflation of two variants:

All my enemies {rejoiced / heard of my trouble,} that you had done it.

Oh bring on . . . ! Many have translated this as imperative, which the context favors, by emending the MT *hēbē'tā* to imperative *hābē';* commonly the Syriac version is cited in favor of the change. Though the result is the same, note that the present translation is based on taking *hēbē'tā* as a case where the perfect is used to express a wish or request, a use that seems to be attested elsewhere in the book; cf. 4:22 and especially 3:55–66 *passim,* where perfects alternate with imperatives and other expressions of volitive ideas. The existence of such a use of the Hebrew perfect is disputed, and even if its existence is acknowledged, the history of such a use and its extent are matters of dispute. Whatever the situation may be for Hebrew generally, it seems best to recognize that the author of Lamentations occasionally uses the perfect to express wishes and requests, rather than to emend away all such occurrences or resort to other explanations. For other discussions of this construction in Hebrew, see Bergsträsser, *Hebräische Grammatik,* II. Teil, para. 6i; Carl Brockelmann, *Grundriss,* II (Berlin, 1908), 29–30; Paul Joüon, *Grammaire de l'Hébreu Biblique,* 2d ed. (Rome, 1947), para. 112k; Mitchell Dahood, "Ugaritic-Hebrew Syntax and Style," *Ugarit-Forschungen* 1 (Neukirchen-Vluyn, 1969), 20, n. 7, and his GRAMMAR OF THE PSALTER, in *Psalms III, 101–150,* The Anchor Bible (AB), vol. 17A (New York, 1970), pp. 414–17.

COMMENT

The first of the five Lamentations is an exceptionally impressive poetic depiction of the desolation of the city of God. From one point of view, the poem is a series of brief pictures of the distress, none sustained for very long, and mostly traditional, derived from the stock images and ideas of Israelite poetic laments. This creates a certain monotony, a notable contribution to this effect being the five-fold repetition of the theme "there is no one to comfort her" (1:2, 9, 16, 17, 21). Thus superficially viewed, the form of the poem is contributed by an external device, the alphabetic acrostic (see Introduction above), there being no easily observable outline or logical progression of thought or action. Such a view, however, misses the poet's intent. His aim, we may infer, was not to write a poem moving to an obvious climax of action or thought, but rather to create one of essentially uniform tone, corresponding to the one appalling catastrophe and the unvarying misery that went with it and followed it. A man who has just lost a wife or child cannot keep his mind off it, and that is how this poet writes, ever returning to the source of his grief.

On the other hand, there is a definite psychological progress in the poem; it moves from an external, objective, third-person view, to an internal, subjective, first-person view. This contributes the movement and organization which are lacking at other levels of the poem. Two persons speak. The first is the poet himself. He writes of Zion in the third person, as one observing from outside what has happened to her, and the reasons for it. This is the point of view through almost exactly half the poem, vss. 1–11. It is broken, however, by the brief ejaculatory prayer at 9c and 11c: "Yahweh, look upon my misery!" These prepare the way for the shift in speaker from vs. 12 on (one could also argue that part two begins at 11c). From this point on it is Zion herself who speaks, and the more detached voice is only occasionally heard (15c, 17). This shift to the point of view of the personified Zion achieves several things. One effect is to heighten the expression of anguish, and to intensify the participation in this anguish by the worshiper when the poem is used liturgically. At the same time the introduction at this point of Zion herself as the speaker is a means by which the poet expresses the central tragedy in the situation. The point of the book is not just that a nation has fallen and that a man, or the survivors as a whole, is grieved, but that a greater thing, a greater person, is in anguish: Zion, the city of God, the community of the elect, who in her historical being is not identical with those alive at any one time. Appropriately, then, the first "I" in the book is not the "I" of an individual, even as the spokesman for the survivors, but of Zion herself. Thus through this personification the poet is able to use very personal, emotional language, but at the same time to transcend the merely subjective. Finally, one may observe that the use of first-person speech by Zion here affects our reaction to the use of first-person forms elsewhere: the use of "I" by the poet himself, or of "we" by the surviving community, and so on. We are prepared by chapter 1 for the appearance of an individual as representative of the people, and for the idea that one person's suffering can depict, or help explain, or even relieve, the suffering of the city of God—a point that becomes especially important for chapter 3.

Outline

A. The anguish of Zion, seen from without.
   1–11 (with brief prayers by Zion herself, 9c and 11c)
B. Zion's anguish, as she herself feels it.
   12–22 (with recurrence of the previous point of view in 15c, 17)

It seems likely that the first poem was intended from the outset for use in congregational worship, like the other poems in the book (see the Introduction). On the other hand, the idea that it received a kind of dramatic performance, with different persons speaking the parts of Zion, of the poet, etc., a hypothesis which has been advanced by Wiesmann and H.-J. Kraus (Kraus does not press the hypothesis) among others, seems speculative in the extreme.

On the date of chapter 1, which is taken here to be the same as
that of the other chapters, see the Introduction. There too the
reader will find a brief discussion of the literary genre or genres to
which this poem belongs, and a defense of the viewpoint adopted
in the present commentary, which is that identification of this poem
as a funeral song or the like tends to hinder rather than advance
understanding of it.

"How" (Heb. *'ēkāh;* elsewhere also *'ēk*) is a traditional way of
beginning a poem which depicts a striking change, from virtue to
vice, for example, Isa 1:21, or often, from a glorious past to a
miserable present. This last use accounts for its frequent occurrence
in laments and funeral songs (cf. 2:1; 4:1; Jer 48:17; Isa 14:4;
Jer 9:19[18H]; Ezek 26:17). The effect is to make of what follows an incredulous question: "How can it be that . . . ?"—an
expression of the speaker's astonishment, grief, or indignation at
what has happened.

The opening stanza (vs. 1) is one of the most carefully worked
out in the book from a formal point of view. The three lines are
parallel to each other (so-called external parallelism). The first two
are linked by repetition of *rabbātī* (a repetition not reproduced in
the present translation) and the third is closely joined to them by
the parallel word *śārātī*. This is, however, placed in a chiastic
position, that is, it is in the opposite position in the line with respect
to its counterpart *rabbātī*. This formal elaborateness marks the importance of the themes introduced. At once we encounter the picture
of Zion as a person, a mourning woman. As stated above, this
becomes of increasing importance throughout the poem, and in other
parts of the book as well. Simultaneously another theme appears,
the contrast of former glories to present desolation and humiliation.
This is a common element in laments and funeral songs ("How the
mighty have fallen!"), but here there is a significant addition. This
lies in the element of hyperbole involved in calling Jerusalem "greatest among nations" and "noblest of states." Aside from its rhetorical
effect, as heightening the contrast, this recalls the extravagant, semi-
mythical language used of Zion in, for example, Ps 48:1–2[2–
3H]: "His holy mountain, beautiful in elevation, the joy of all the
earth, Mount Zion, on the slopes of Zaphon." This language belongs
to description of Jerusalem, not as she ever was in fact, but as she
was in the eyes of those who believed her to be the city of God. We
have here, then, a less explicit anticipation of the question of 2:15:

"Is this the city they call the perfection of beauty" (or ". . . the joy of all the earth?"; see NOTE ad loc.). Jerusalem is compared to a widow because widows, together with orphans, were the most defenseless people in ancient society (cf. 5:3; Isa 49:20–21; 51:18; 54:4–6), and the most to be pitied.

The next stanza (vs. 2) continues the personification, but adds a new theme—Zion as the faithless woman. Thereby another major concern of the book is given early announcement: why did it happen? By using an ambiguous image the poet manages to stress two different elements: the pathos of the situation, and the nature of Zion's guilt. When it is said "All her friends have betrayed her," this is what is commonly said in laments: that the sufferer's friends have forsaken him and become hostile (Ps 88:18[19H]; 38:11 [12H]); cf. also the Babylonian "Poem of the Righteous Sufferer" (*Ludlul bēl nēmeqi*), Tablet I, lines 84–88: "My friend has become foe," etc., W. G. Lambert, *Babylonian Wisdom Literature* [Oxford, 1960], p. 35). The lovers and friends in the present case are figurative, however, for the faithless allies of Israel. In the metaphorical language familiar especially from Hosea, Jeremiah, and Ezekiel, Israel, the wife of Yahweh, has been unfaithful to him by entering into alliance with other nations and gods (e.g., Hosea 8:9–10; Ezek 16:28–29; 23:5–21). These paramours in the end forsake her (Hosea 2:9[7H]); Jer 22:20–22; 30:14) or turn against her (Ezek 16:37–41; 23:22–29; cf. also vs. 19 below). Because only Yahweh was supposed to be Israel's overlord, and the one who protected her and fought her battles, the prophets regarded it as the most serious kind of apostasy when Israel put herself under the rule of some earthly kingdom. This point of view is fully shared by the writer of Lamentations: cf. 5:6–7.

If the Hebrew of vs. 3 is correctly translated here (see the NOTE), the whole verse refers to Judah's troubles in the time before the final collapse. Even though she "dwelt among the nations," that is, existed as an independent nation, she did not in her latter days enjoy "rest." The last word is of considerable weight: "rest" in the Promised Land was an important part of Israel's conception of what belonged to her as God's people, and its removal was a sign that his favor had departed. On "rest" compare 5:5 and Gerhard von Rad, "There Remains Still a Rest for the People of God: An Investigation of a Biblical Conception," in *The Problem of the Hexateuch and Other Essays* (Edinburgh and London, 1966), pp. 94–102.

The elements mentioned in vs. 4 combine reasonably well to depict desolate Jerusalem as deprived of religious festivals. The highways mourn, lacking any pilgrims, and the gates, the focus of festive coming and going, are deserted. The priests, once vitally active at the great feasts, now sigh. To account for mention of the "virgins," commentators have pointed, with some plausibility, to mention of virgins or young women as having a role in festal celebrations, for example, Jer 31:13 and Judg 21:19–21. With "and she is bitter," the personified Zion is again the subject. One may go further, however, and suggest that the poet's picture has been shaped, whether he was conscious of it or not, by traditional descriptions of ritual mourning, specifically in time of drought. The theme "the land mourns in drought" appears in longer and shorter forms at numerous points in biblical literature. Typical elements include, first, the statement that the land "mourns" or "is dried up" (Heb. *'ābal;* cf. Joel 1:10; Jer 14:2; Hosea 4:3). The alternative translations are given because Heb. *'ābal* means both; lexicographers disagree as to whether one root or two is involved, see KB³, s.v.; Joseph Scharbert, *Der Schmerz im Alten Testament,* Bonner Biblische Beiträge 8 (Bonn, 1955), pp. 47–58; cf. also Norbert Lohfink, "Enthielten die im Alten Testament bezeugten Klageriten eine Phase des Schweigens?" VT 12 (1962), 274–75. The question need not concern us here, for there can be no doubt that speakers of Hebrew associated the two, even if only as homonyms, so that even in a context where the meaning "to dry up" is appropriate, associations with "mourning" are present. In examples of the topos under consideration, not only the earth is said to mourn (dry up), but also "gates," as in the present passage; compare Jer 14:2; Isa 3:26; Lam 2:8. In this sort of description, there is commonly found a listing of what has been taken away; for example, birds, beasts, and even fish, Hosea 4:3; cattle and birds, Jer 12:4; vintagers, etc., Isa 16:10. This element is perhaps present in the "none come in for the feasts" of the present verse. When nature mourns, people also mourn; either the same verb *'ābal* is used (Joel 1:9) or the closely associated term *'umlal* (Hosea 4:3; cf. Isa 19:8); or the mourning activity is otherwise described: Jer 14:2; Isa 3:26; Isa 19:8. The priests, mentioned as sighing in the passage under discussion, appear prominently in Joel 1:9, 13, where they are urged to mourn and weep. In the same passage (Joel 1:8) one discovers, in a simile, a parallel to the "virgins" here in vs. 4: "Lament like a virgin girded with sackcloth for the husband of her youth." Jer 31:12–14 depicts a glorious time when "I will turn their mourning into joy," and is a kind of mirror-image of the mourning topos: grain, wine, and oil and the young of flocks and herds are promised along with plentiful water, the virgins will rejoice in the dance, and the priests will have great abundance to eat. It is obvious that a very similar assembly of elements has gone into making up the description. If one pushes still further back, one may propose that the elements brought together in this literary theme were orig- inally associated with the mourning for the dead god of fertility, for example, the Canaanite Baal, who has disappeared during the heat of summer, along with all life and growth. The mourning for such a figure is referred to in Ezek 8:14; Zech 12:10–14, and is depicted with considerable fullness in the Baal epic, for which see ANET, p. 138 (I* AB vi 9–22=CTA 5; UT 67), where the Virgin (*btlt*) Anat is the principal mourner, ANET, pp. 139–40 (I AB i 1–18= CTA 6; UT 49+62). (On echoes of the Canaanite myth in the Old Testament, with specific reference to Joel 1:8, see H. W. Wolff on Joel [in Biblischer Kommentar], with references to studies by F. F. Hvidberg, A. S. Kapelrud, and Miloš Bič.) For a fuller discussion, see the writer's article in *Perspective* 12 (1971), 121–33.

As used by the writer of Lamentations, this originally mytholog- ical theme is modified almost beyond recognition, and one need not suppose that the writer was himself aware of all the overtones of his imagery when seen in the light of its history. Nevertheless, it seems worth the effort to trace that history, even at the cost of digressing from the theme of the poem, for it illuminates the way in which the author's mind worked. He was very strongly under the influence of inherited literary patterns, in both obvious and subtle ways. He is very far from giving us a journalist's account of what took place; if he was an observer of the siege and the beginning of the captivity, as seems likely, then he has cast his observations into inherited, age-old forms—in fact, it would at some points be correct to say that the traditional literary forms determined his perceptions and memories of the events.

"Her enemies came out on top" (vs. 5) would be, in a more literal rendering, "Her enemies have become the head," an allusion to: "He [the alien in Israel's midst] will become the head, and you will become the tail" (Deut 28:44, cf. 28:13). An ancient midrash on Lamentations already connects the two: "Had you been worthy, you would have read in the Torah, 'And the Lord will make thee the head,' but now that you are unworthy, you read, 'Her adversaries are become the head'" (translation of A. Cohen, *Midrash Rabbah,* eds. H. Freedman and Maurice Simon, Vol. VIII [London, 1939], 16). Thus this line indicates that the writer may have seen in the fate of Jerusalem the fulfillment of a threat, or curse, associated with the covenant with God. This same insight finds indirect expression elsewhere in the book; cf. 4:3–4, 10; 5:18, and possibly also 1:8; 2:16; 3:10–11; 4:6; 5:14–15. Deut 28 and Lev 26, both of which come at the end of lists of obligations imposed by the covenant with God, are the clearest biblical examples of the association of curses with covenant. On covenant forms in the ancient Near East and the Old Testament, see George Mendenhall, *Law and Covenant in Israel and in the Ancient Near East,* Pittsburgh, 1955; the role of the curses is treated on p. 34 there, and more fully in D. R. Hillers, *Treaty-Curses and the Old Testament Prophets,* Rome, 1964.

The second line (vs. 5b) continues and makes more explicit the covenant image implied in the first. Zion's sin is "rebellion," *peša',* a term which, although it is often used of sin against God, is originally derived from political life, where it is a common term for revolt against a suzerain (II Kings 1:1; 3:5, etc.); it seems best to suppose that the word retains that connotation here. Since the first two lines of the stanza have alluded to covenant ideas, one is perhaps justified in detecting a similar note in the third line, with its reference to exile. That the populace was led captive to Babylon is, of course, a statement of fact, but in the context of this stanza one may suppose that the poet means to recall that this also was one of the curses threatened for breach of covenant (cf. Deut 28:36, 63–68, and Hillers, *Treaty-Curses,* pp. 33–34). The personification of Zion is brought to the fore again in the reference to the inhabitants of Judah as "her children."

The following stanza (vs. 6), loosely joined to the preceding by "and" (*waw*-consecutive, see NOTE) is not closely linked with the foregoing in thought, but perhaps the idea of the children going away into exile suggested to the writer the departure of the glory of Israel with which the new stanza begins. After the general statement of line 1 follows a specific detail: the princes have been driven to the point of collapse, the idea being that this happened during the siege and flight from Jerusalem, or perhaps on the long road into captivity. The fate of the princes is cast in the form of a simile involving either "stags," MT: *'ayyālīm,* or "rams," *'ēlīm,* implied by Greek and Vulgate; the same consonantal text permits either interpretation. It is preferable to take this word as "stags," since the third line seems to be a continuation of the simile, and the hunting image fits better with "stags" than "rams." (For *rādap* in the sense "to hunt" cf. I Sam 26:20.) The enemy is compared to a hunter also in 3:52 and Jer 16:16. J. Rimbach has called my attention to a parallel in one of the curses of Esarhaddon's vassal-treaties (lines 576–78): "Just as a stag is chased and killed, so may your avengers chase and kill you, your brothers, your sons" (translation of E. Reiner, ANET, p. 540). The simile is effective, not only within this stanza, but as a link to the last line of the preceding verse, since "before the hunter" echoes "before the enemy."

Part of Jerusalem's suffering was that, in her utter helplessness, her enemies laughed when they saw her (vs. 7). This is a common motif in a variety of Old Testament contexts. It is used of an individual in Lam 3:14 and Ps 37:13; 52:6[8H]; Prov 1:26; Job 30:1. From use of individuals it is transferred to nations, and occurs in laments for the community in Ps 44:14; 79:4; 80:7[6H]; cf. Jer 48:26, 39.

If vs. 8 is correctly translated here (see NOTE), the picture of vs. 7 is carried on: Zion in her misery is the butt of scorn, expressed by derisive shaking of the head. There is a certain intensification since here it is not just the enemy who laughs, but all who once respected her. Even if it is correct to keep the reading *nīdāh* ("object of scorn," lit. "nodding"; see NOTE) the writer may have intended a pun on a word of similar sound, *niddāh,* "menstruous, unclean thing," for he introduces as the reason for the scorn that her revilers "saw her naked." (Cf. Gordis, ad loc.) The same two ideas, exposure of nakedness (*'erwāh*) and uncleanness (*niddāh*) are associated in Lev 20:21 (cf. Ezek 22:10), hence it seems unlikely that the sequence here is entirely fortuitous. The motif "they saw her naked" is meaningful at three levels. It is primarily an expression of the utter contempt with which Zion is treated. Exposure of one's body, especially the genitals, was to the ancient Israelites an almost immeasurable disgrace, a shame they felt much more deeply than most moderns would. This attitude finds expression in the story of Noah's drunkenness (Gen 9:20–27) and in several idioms: "uncover the nakedness of so-and-so" is an expression for "enter into incestuous marriage" (Lev 18:6–18; 20: 11–21), and "something exposed" is an idiom for something indecent in Deut 23:14[15H]; 24:1. Hence stripping was apparently part of the cruel treatment that might be meted out to a prostitute (Ezek 16:35–39; 23:29; cf. Isa 3:17), and is used metaphorically, of the punishment of nations (Isa 47:2–3; Lam 4:21; Nahum 3:5). This is the most obvious meaning of the line, but in addition one may note that being stripped bare is also a curse connected with treaties or covenants (see COMMENT on vs. 5 above), and the writer may have intended to allude once again to the notion that Israel's punishment followed justly and inevitably on breach of her covenant with God. Finally, one may note that the expression "to see the nakedness" of a country is used (Gen 42: 9, 12) of spying out its weakness from a strategic point of view, and it is possible that a play on this sense of the term is also involved here.

"Pollution," ritual uncleanness, is a not very euphemistic reference to menstrual blood (cf. Isa 64:6[5H]), but the exact point of the image—assuming that the writer had something very specific in mind—is difficult to determine. One finds elsewhere the idea that the innocent blood shed in a city makes it unclean (Ps 106:38–39 and cf. COMMENT on 4:13–15 below); perhaps that is the idea here, but nothing in the immediate context prepares for it. Elsewhere one finds the notion that "whoredom" with idols or other nations makes the land (pictured as a woman) unclean, ritually impure; thus Hosea 5:3; 6:10; Jer 2:23; Ezek 23:7, 13.

"She did not think of the consequences for her" (9a) seems to have no very close connection to the first half of the line. The identical words are used of Babylon, also in a poem where she is personified as a humiliated woman, Isa 47:7. The point there is that she had always thought she would be a queen, and did not give a moment's thought to the consequences of her actions. Hence this half-line seems to be tied more closely to the second line of the stanza, with its reference to the fall of Jerusalem, than to the foregoing. The verb *yārad*, "to come down," is used of the humiliation of persons in Ezek 30:6 and Isa 47:1 and that is evidently the sense intended here also, the personification being continued. Note, however, that the verb is also used of the fall of a besieged city in Deut 20:20. Heb. *pᵉlā'îm* (translated "astonishingly" here) does not occur elsewhere in this form or this kind of usage, and the exact nuance escapes us. Perhaps the idea is similar to that of 4:12: in view of Yahweh's promises, no one could believe that the enemy would take Jerusalem. Here, however, it is Jerusalem herself who did not believe that retribution awaited her. The verses close with a prayer which, as stated above, is to be thought of as spoken by the city herself, an anticipation of the shift in point of view which is carried out completely in vs. 12.

The heathen have reached out greedily for Zion's "precious things," which refers in this context to the temple treasures, which the Babylonians took away, II Kings 25:13–17. The command referred to in the following lines is obviously Deut 23:3[4H], in view of the close verbal agreement: "No Ammonite or Moabite shall enter the assembly of Yahweh; not even the tenth generation of them shall enter the assembly of Yahweh, ever." Since the Babylonians (Chaldaeans) were the ones who entered the temple, and since there is no evidence that Moabites and Ammonites figured in the destruction of Jerusalem at this time, it is evident that the Deuteronomic command has been broadened, if only by poetic license, to cover the "heathen," *gōyîm,* in general. (Later, in the time of Ezra and Nehemiah, the command was applied to all non-Israelites, and was taken as prohibiting intermarriage; see Neh 13:1–3.) Here in Lamentations, the reference to the commandment is made with ironic intention: no heathen was to enter, even piously and peaceably, into the sacred assembly, but now they break in violently and rob the holy place.

The final verse of this first half of the poem (11) reaches a climax of pathos. In order to get food, the survivors of the siege have sold their "darlings," that is, children, as explained already by Theodoret (died ca. A.D. 460). Heb. *maḥᵃmaddēhem* (Qre; Ktib is probably meant to be *maḥᵃmūdēhem*) means "precious things," and may be used of possessions or treasures, as in vs. 10, but is used also of "precious children, darlings," for example, in Hosea 9:16: "Even though they give birth, I will slay the darling offspring of their wombs," *maḥᵃmaddē biṭnām.* Compare the expression *maḥᵃmaddē 'ayin,* which may refer to things, as in I Kings 20:6, or to people, Ezek 24:16; Lam 2:4. The picture of the Israelites giving up mere possessions to stay alive lacks poignancy. That they gave up children to buy food is both more striking and better paralleled in ancient descriptions of famine, on which see especially A. L. Oppenheim, "'Siege-Documents' from Nippur," *Iraq* 17 (1955), 69–89. Compare also the *Atra-ḫasīs* epic, where in a description of a great famine there occur the lines: "The daughter watched the scales (at the sale) of the mother. The mother watched the scales (at the sale) of the daughter"; translation of W. G. Lambert and A. R. Millard, *Atra-ḫasīs* (Oxford, 1969), p. 113, the lines quoted being their manuscript S, Rev. vi, lines 9–10. Like vs. 9, so also 11 closes with a brief prayer, spoken by Jerusalem. It seems likely that the poet meant to begin a new section precisely at the middle of his poem (vs. 12); otherwise one could also regard this prayer in 11c as beginning the second part of the poem.

Zion herself speaks now, and throughout almost all the rest of the poem. This climactic half of the chapter begins with a stanza which is appropriately general in its terms: all are urged to look and consider: "Is there any pain like my pain?" The detailed exposition of what the pain consists in, of what specifically Yahweh has done to her, is to be set forth in following verses. This reference to those who pass by is an exceedingly common motif in Old Testament literature. Usually it is as in Lam 2:15 (see COMMENT there): those who pass by will mock, etc. Here the sense is somewhat different, the best biblical parallel being Job 21:29, where Job, in response to the notion that the wicked suffer, asserts the contrary: "Haven't you asked those who pass on the road?" The passersby are a figurative representation of common human experience, the additional implication being that they are unbiased because uninvolved in what they see.

The intensification of feeling which is characteristic of the second half of the poem is noticeable already here in vs. 12. In part one, it is plainly stated only once (5b) that Yahweh is the one who has afflicted Zion, but from vs. 12 on this sort of statement is much more frequent. Yahweh has brought to pass "the day of his burning anger." The idea of a *dies irae,* a day of wrath belonging to Yahweh, is very widely attested in the Old Testament, beginning as early as Amos, nearly two hundred years before the present passage was written. Scholars disagree as to exactly what the Israelite conception—or conceptions—of the day of Yahweh was at various times. The book of Lamentations is notable in that it several times (here and 2:1, 21, 22) refers to the day of Yahweh's wrath as *past.* The awful events of the siege and fall were already a decisive outpouring of Yahweh's wrath, a judgment day. (The author still looks for a future "day" of vengeance on the enemy, however; see vs. 21.)

The reference to "fire" in the first line of 13 constitutes a link to vs. 12, with its *burning* anger." The picture of pain as fire shut up in one's bones occurs in a famous passage in Jeremiah (20:9). This and the following verse describe Zion's plight entirely in terms of the suffering of an individual, with language drawn from the repertory of biblical laments. Only in vs. 15 is there again reference to an actual event in the siege of Jerusalem. Actually, this consistent mode of presentation begins at vs. 12, where only the phrase "day of his burning anger" is a reference to the event.

Zion's trouble is like a net or trap which was spread out in her path and which has ensnared her. This is an exceptionally common image in the Old Testament. God himself is said to spread a net for men here and in Jer 50:24; Ezek 12:13; 17:20; 32:3; Hosea 7:12; cf. also Ps 94:13. "He turned me back" follows naturally on the image of the net in that it also is based on the comparison of a man's way of life to walking along a path—the divine punishment is a checking of a man's walking; cf. Isa 28:13 for a similar association of ideas. "Desolate" and "sick" emphasize the subjective aspect of the suffering, rather than the objective destruction, since closely parallel passages: Isa 1:5; Jer 8:18; Lam 1:22 and 5:17, specifically refer to the "heart" as sick.

God has kept watch over his people's steps (see the NOTE for this translation), not to guard them but to trip them up. The idea is similar to that of 3:9: "he has made my paths crooked," and 3:10–11, where Yahweh is said to lie in wait like a bear or lion.

Next the poet presents the destruction of Jerusalem, especially of the people, as a grim harvest. (If the difficult first word of vs. 15 is correctly translated as "heap up"—see the NOTE—the whole verse maintains this theme.) Like sheaves stacked in the middle of the threshing-floor, so the mighty men of Zion were gathered up in her midst. Then Yahweh called her enemies together to crush them. Similar harvest imagery is used of destruction or punishment in Jer 9:22[21H]; 51:33; Amos 1:3; Micah 4:12–13 ("For he has gathered them like sheaves to the threshing-floor. Arise and thresh!"); Isa 41:15–16. Note that in Joel 3[4H]:13 the picture of the grain harvest is followed by the image of the vintage, as here; the sequence was probably influenced by the order in the agricultural year. The lengthy, vivid expansion of this image of the "grapes of wrath" in Isa 63:1–6 makes explicit what is to be understood in the laconic statement of Lamentations. This first-person section of the chapter closes with the picture of mother Zion weeping, and the familiar theme recurs; "any comforter is far from me" (vs. 16).

At vs. 17 there is a shift in emphasis, signaled by the momentary abandonment of first person in favor of third person, that is, the poet speaks about Zion, instead of Zion speaking for herself. Though Zion soon reappears, the rest of the poem is made different from what went before by two themes which may be said to dominate, even though the content of 17–22 is extremely varied and though there are agitated shifts from description of troubles to complaint, to appeals for sympathy, and so on (for comments on individual verses, see also the NOTES). One new theme is a progressive turning toward Yahweh. In vs. 17 it is established that he is the author of the calamity, and in vs. 18 comes a confession that he is justified in what he has done. "Yahweh is in the right" is an expression ultimately derived from legal language; it is the formula for pronouncing a verdict. Unexpressed here, but implied, is the other half of the formula, ". . . and I am in the wrong." The following "for I disobeyed his command" supplies the basis for the verdict. Compare Exod 9:27; I Sam 24:17[18H]; II Kings 10:9; Ps 119:137; Ezra 9:15. In religious language it is a formula for expressing humble submission to divine judgment; cf. especially Neh 9:33: "You are in the right with respect to all that has come upon us, for you have kept your word whereas we have behaved wrongly." Continuing this turning toward Yahweh, the last three verses are dominated by appeals to him to see (20), to hear (21), and finally (21–22) to bring retribution on the enemy (see the NOTE for translation of 21c as a prayer). This retribution is to take the form of a "day" of judgment on the enemies. The assumption made is that Yahweh's sway is universal, and what he has already brought on Israel, "the day of his burning anger" (vs. 12), should also come on those who laughed at her fall. Cf. 3:58–66 and 4:21–22.

The second dominant characteristic of this final portion of the poem is the recurrence of statements made earlier. "Realize my pain" (18) echoes 12a and b; "My young men and women have been taken prisoner" is a modification of 5c; "I called for my lovers" recalls vs. 2; "I groan" restates vs. 8: "She groans," and still other examples could be added. This echoing is frequently in first person, contrasting with the third person of the original statement. The effect of this device is comparable to that of a composer's restatement, at the end of a movement, of the themes with which he began, modified and intensified. Following this coda the poem comes to a quiet close: "For many are my groans, and my heart is sick."

II
"The Lord became like an enemy"
(2:1–22)

Aleph   1 How the Lord in his anger has treated Zion
with contempt!
He has thrown down from heaven to earth
the glory of Israel.
He had no regard for his footstool on the
day of his wrath.

Beth   2 The Lord consumed, unsparingly, all the
dwellings of Jacob.
He tore down, in his anger, the fortresses
of Judah.
He brought down to earth, he profaned,
her king and princes.

Gimel   3 In fierce anger he lopped off the horns of Israel.
He turned back his right hand in the face
of the enemy,
And he burned against Jacob like a fire that
consumes on every side.

Daleth   4 He bent his bow like an enemy; the sword-hilt
was in his right hand.
Like a foe <he smote> and slew all the
good-looking men.
On the tents of Zion he poured out his
wrath like fire.

He   5 The Lord became an enemy; he consumed
Israel.
He consumed all his citadels; he destroyed
his fortresses.

He made moaning and mourning plentiful
in Judah.

Waw   6 He laid waste his covert like a garden; he
ruined his assembly.

Yahweh made festival and sabbath to be
forgotten in Zion,

And in his fierce anger he poured contempt
on king and priest.

Zayin   7 Yahweh rejected his own altar; he spurned his
sanctuary.

He gave over to the enemy the walls of her
citadels.

They made a noise in the house of Yahweh
as though it were a feast day.

Heth   8 Yahweh planned to destroy the wall of Zion.

He stretched out the line; he did not relent
from slaughtering.

So he made rampart and wall mourn;
together they languished.

Teth   9 Her gates have sunk into the earth; he destroyed
their bars.

Her king and her princes are among
the heathen; there is no instruction;

Also her prophets find no vision from
Yahweh.

Yod   10 In silence they sit on the ground, the elders of
Zion.

They put dirt on their heads; they wear
sackcloth.

The virgins of Jerusalem bow their heads
to the ground.

Kaph   11 My eyes are worn out with tears; my bowels
churn.

My liver is poured out on the ground at the
destruction of my people.

As the child and the baby were fainting in
the streets of the city,

Lamed	12 They said to their mothers, "Where is grain and wine?"
	As they fainted like wounded men in the streets of the city,
	As they breathed their last in their mothers' laps.
Mem	13 To what can I liken, to what compare you, O Jerusalem?
	What likeness can I use to comfort you, O fair Zion?
	For your ruin is vast as the sea—who could mend you?
Nun	14 Your prophets saw visions for you that were mere whitewash.
	They did not lay bare your sin, to make things better again,
	But they saw for you oracles that were empty deceptions.
Samekh	15 All who pass along the road clap hands at you;
	They whistle and shake their heads at Jerusalem.
	"Is this the city they call the perfection of beauty?"
Pe	16 They open wide their mouths at you, all your enemies;
	They whistle and gnash their teeth; they say "We have consumed them!
	Yes, this is the day we waited for! We have actually seen it!"
Ayin	17 Yahweh has done what he planned; he has carried out what he said he would,
	What he commanded from olden times: He tore down without sparing
	And he made your enemies happy at your expense; He raised high the horns of your foes.

Sade   18 Cry from the heart to the Lord, O remorseful
                Zion!
            Shed tears like a torrent night and day.
            Give yourself no relief! Do not let your
                eyes be still!

Qof   19 Arise, cry out at night, as each watch begins.
            Pour out your heart like water before the
                face of the Lord.
            Lift up your hands to him for the lives of
                your children.

            . . . .

Resh   20 "Look, Yahweh, and consider whom you have
                treated so.
            Should women eat what they bore, the
                children they have raised?
            Should priest and prophet be slain in the
                sanctuary of the Lord?

Shin   21 Out in the streets on the ground they lie, boys
                and old men.
            My young men and women have fallen by
                the sword.
            You killed them on the day of your wrath;
                you slaughtered without mercy.

Taw   22 You invited, as though to a festival, men to
                attack me from all sides,
            So that, on the day of Yahweh's wrath,
                there were none who escaped or got
                away—
            My enemies have wiped out those whom I
                cherished and brought up."

NOTES

2:1. *has treated . . . with contempt!* MT *yāʿīb* is traditionally taken as a denominative verb from *ʿāb,* "cloud," and translated "cover with clouds" (so also Albrektson and others in modern times). But this explanation of the *hapax legomenon* is suspiciously *ad hoc,* and the meaning is not especially suited to this context, nor is "beclouding" otherwise an image for punishment. Ehrlich, Rudolph, and others have explained the word as related to an Ar. *ʿāba,* "to blame, revile," and translate: "How the Lord . . . has *disgraced* Zion" which fits the context well. As an alternate suggestion, one may propose (following in most respects McDaniel, *Biblica* 49 [1968], 34–35) that the text be vocalized *yōʿīb,* as if from a root *wʿb, to which is related the noun *tōʿēbāh* ("abomination"; on the derivation see W. F. Albright, *From the Stone Age to Christianity* [Baltimore, 1957], p. 176, n. 45) and the denominative verb *tʿb. yōʿīb* would be equal in sense to *tāʿēb* as in Ps 106:40: "And the anger of Yahweh was aroused at his people, and he treated with contempt (*wayᵉtāʿēb*) his inheritance." Although *wʿb would be the original root of *tōʿēbāh,* the Hiphil *hōʿīb* might well be a denominative, a back-formation from the noun; cf. *hōdāh* from *tōdāh* as explained by W. F. Albright, "The Names 'Israel' and 'Judah' with an Excursus on the Etymology of *tōdā* and *tōrāh,*" *Journal of Biblical Literature* 46 (1927), 151–85. Note that the Targum has a form of *qwṣ,* "despise." See further at 4:1, NOTE.

Zion. "Daughter Zion"; see Introduction.

his footstool. This is a reference to Zion or the temple as the symbol of the presence of God. It is not a reference to the ark as Albrektson claims (though that may be the case in I Chron 28:2), since the ark was not destroyed in 587 B.C., but much earlier, unless Jer 3:16 is a later interpolation in Jeremiah. The intention of this image seems to be to describe in a reverent, modest way the mode of God's presence: his throne is in heaven, that is, his dwelling is transcendent and remote, but he is nevertheless present in a special way in his temple, the place where his feet touch.

2. *dwellings.* Heb. *nᵉ'ōt* is used of pastures, and also of the dwellings of men. The latter sense has been preferred here because the verb *billa'*, "he consumed," is used elsewhere in this chapter with buildings as its object (vss. 5, 8), and because a reference to buildings seems to fit better in the context of the verse.

Judah. "Daughter Judah"; see Introduction.

her king and princes. MT *mamlākāh wᵉśārehā* literally rendered as it stands, would be "a kingdom and its (her) princes." A translation "her king and princes" (so LXX) can be defended in various ways; for a detailed discussion, with references, see McDaniel, *Biblica* 49 (1968), 35–36. Instead of recognizing here a noun *mamlākāh*, "prince," as Albright does, comparing Phoen. *mmlkt,* the present writer prefers to suppose that the initial *m* of MT *mamlākāh* was originally an enclitic *mem* attached to the preceding verb, *ḥillēl* (on this particle, see the NOTE at 3:17), yielding a text: *ḥillēl-m malkāh wᵉśārehā;* cf. vs. 9b.

profaned for *ḥillēl* is based on Ps 79:40; vss. 39–46 of the psalm resemble the present context in other respects also. Otherwise (as suggested to me by D. N. Freedman) one might translate "wounded."

3. *he lopped off the horns of Israel.* The meaning is "He destroyed all Israel's proud strength." "Horn" as a metaphor for strength and pride is extremely frequent in the Old Testament and occurs in other ancient Near Eastern literature as well; see Édouard Paul Dhorme, "L'emploi métaphorique des noms de parties du corps en hébreu et en akkadien," *Revue biblique* 29 (1920), 465–506; 30 (1921), 374–99, 517–40; 31 (1922), 215–33, 489–547; 32 (1923), 185–212. Close parallels to the present passage are Jer 48:25; Ps 75:10[11H].

his right hand. The pronoun probably refers to Israel, not God. God destroys the "horn" of Israel in 3a, and here turns back Israel's right hand—both parts of the body, symbolic of strength, belong to Israel.

like a fire. Hebrew has *kᵉ'ēš lehābāh*, "like a fire of flame." Since this seems to make the first colon too long, *lehābāh* is to be

deleted, either as an addition made because the construct phrase
was such a frequently used idiom (e.g. Isa 4:5) or as a variant
reading which has been incorporated in the text (cf. NOTE on 5:5).

4. The text is suspect at several points. *niṣṣāb yᵉmīnō*, literally
"his right hand (fem.) is stationed" (masc. adj.) can scarcely be
correct. If *kᵉṣār*, "like a foe," is added to the end of line 1, the
line is made rather long, and line 2 is too short, but if it is
put with line 2, the result is an impossible "like a foe and he
slew." The present translation is based on understanding *niṣṣāb*
as the noun "(sword-)hilt" as in Judg 3:22, as suggested to the
present writer by J. Rimbach, and on restoring a *b* ("in"; lost by
haplography?) before *yᵉmīnō*. For parallels to the picture of God
as a warrior who draws a bow and wields a sword (not simultaneously, of course!) see Ps 7:13; Zech 9:13; cf. Isa 41:2; Ps 37:14.
In the second line *kᵉṣār*, "like a foe," is a good parallel to
kᵉᵓōyēb, but a verb has dropped out after it, perhaps *hikkāh*,
"he smote," to judge from the association of *hikkāh* and *hārag*
in Isa 27:7 and Ps 136:17–18. If *hikkāh* or a verb of similar
meaning is restored at this point, the resulting line exhibits a
syntactic pattern common in Lamentations; see the NOTE on 1:6.

good-looking men. Literally, "those desirable to the eye," used
elsewhere of people (Ezek 24:16) and of precious things (I Kings
20:6). Cf. the COMMENT on 1:11.

Zion. "Daughter Zion"; see Introduction.

5. *his.* MT gives feminine suffix with "citadels"; masculine with
"fortresses." The first is changed to masculine here, following some
other commentators.

Judah. "Daughter Judah"; see Introduction. To 5c compare
"Lamentation over the Destruction of Sumer and Ur," ANET, p.
617, lines 361–62: "The desolate city—in its midst there was
uttered (nothing but) laments (and) dirges, / In its midst there
was uttered (nothing but) laments (and) dirges." So also p. 619,
lines 486–87.

6. The first line is translated here as literally as possible. If
the MT is correct, which is most doubtful, the point might be:
Yahweh laid waste his "covert," that is, the temple (cf. Ps 27:5)
and ruined his (place of) festal assembly (*mōᵃdō*; Morris Jastrow,
ZAW 15, 1895, compares Ps 74:4 for this meaning of *mōʿēd*).
The Targum already recognized this sense in the present verse.
One can point to passages likening the ruin of a people to the

ruining of a vineyard, notably Isa 5:5–6 and also Jer 5:10; 12:10, and the verb *šiḥḥēt*, which is used here (or Hiphil *hišḥīt*), occurs in such contexts. Even so, this interpretation is obviously forced at several points, and is retained here only for want of something better. Most commentators have suggested some sort of emendation, often employing in some way the ambiguous evidence of the versions, but of the many proposals, none seems thoroughly convincing. Albrektson (who defends MT) and McDaniel, *Biblica* 49 (1968), 36–38, treat the passage at length and refer to previous discussions.

7. *her citadels.* The pronoun "her" is retained here on the supposition that it refers to Zion (cf. vs. 6). An emendation to "his" citadels produces consistency in the verse, but would make it necessary to explain what are the "citadels of Yahweh." Citadels (*'armᵉnōt*) are not elsewhere said to belong to Yahweh.

as though it were a feast day. Cf. Hosea 12:10.

8. *Zion.* "Daughter Zion"; see Introduction.

He stretched out the line. Stretching a line is the action of a builder, done to mark straight lines. It is occasionally used, as here, as a metaphor for divine judgment. It is not completely clear how a phrase from the vocabulary of building becomes a synonym for destruction, but it may be that the idea is of a strict, predetermined measure from which God will not deviate; cf. II Kings 21:13; Isa 28:17; 34:11. Brunet, *Les Lamentations contre Jérémie,* pp. 189–98, reaches a similar conclusion in an extensive treatment of the figure; he compares modern use of a balance as a symbol of justice.

rampart and wall. Cf. Isa 26:1.

9. MT has another verb: "he destroyed and shattered her gatebars." Since this makes a rather long second colon, it is possible that the MT is a conflation of variant readings, as occasionally occurs elsewhere in this book (see the NOTE on 5:5). So also Gordis, ad loc. There seems to be no decisive reason for choosing one reading in preference to the other.

10. *In silence.* Heb. *dāmam* means "be silent" in some passages, but in others it probably means "to wail, mourn"; here, as in some other contexts, either meaning is appropriate. For a summary of the problem, with references to extended treatments, see McDaniel, *Biblica* 49 (1969), 38–40.

11. *the destruction of my people.* Literally "the breaking of (the daughter of; see Introduction) my people," an expression

which has its closest parallels in Jeremiah (6:14; 8:11, 21; cf. 14:17). Also similar are Amos 6:6; Isa 30:26.

12. *and wine.* Budde and others have objected to "and wine" on the ground that little children would not have asked for an alcoholic beverage, but this is hyper-critical.

13. *Liken.* Reading *'e'erōk* with Vulgate (*cui comparabo te*) for MT *'a'īdēk,* "testify," as proposed by Johannes Meinhold, ZAW 15 (1895), 286. The pattern of synonymous verbs, joined by *waw,* sharing an object, is a favorite one in the book; cf., for example, 3:2. *'ārak* is associated with *dāmāh* also in Isa 40:18 and Ps 89:6[7H].

13. *Jerusalem.* "Daughter Jerusalem"; see Introduction.

fair Zion. "Virgin daughter Zion"; see Introduction.

14. *mere whitewash.* Heb. *šāw' wetāpēl,* literally "emptiness and whitewash," as applied to visions by false prophets, is best explained by the more extended figure in Ezek 13:10–16, where prophets of peace are compared to men who would whitewash over a rickety wall; cf. also Ezek 22:28.

oracles that were empty deceptions. maś'ōt šāw' ūmaddūḥīm is as it stands a construct chain, perfectly acceptable Hebrew in itself, but such as to make it hard to read this as 3+2 (*"Qinah"* meter). Hence Budde (followed recently by Kraus) wished to repoint the first word as absolute *maśśā'ōt,* and take the following as appositives. This makes the sense of the first colon too flat, however. Rudolph proposes emending to (otherwise unattested) *maśśā'ōt,* "deceptions." It seems better to retain MT and alter one's metrical theory to fit.

15. MT adds, after "perfection of beauty," another epithet, "The joy of the whole earth." This makes the line too long. Since *šeyyō'merū,* "they call," or "of which they said," is necessary to the syntax, one is compelled to choose between the two epithets for Zion. "The perfection of beauty" occurs as an epithet for Tyre (Ezek 27:3), and almost identical epithets are used of the king of Tyre (Ezek 28:12) and of Zion (Ps 50:2). "The joy of the whole earth" recurs (in only slightly different form) as a title of Mount Zion in Ps 48:2[3H]; cf. also Jer 51:41. It may be that MT is a conflation of variant versions of the line; there is no firm basis for preferring one reading to the other.

17. On the horn metaphor, see NOTE at vs. 3.

18. Translation of the first line is based on conjectural emendation of MT. Literally rendered, MT is "Their heart cried out to the

Lord, the wall of Zion" ("daughter Zion," see Introduction), which
is obviously unsatisfactory. For *ṣā'aq* (perfect) read *ṣa'ᵃqī* (fem.
sing. imperative), as many have proposed. *libbām* is understood
as "(from) the heart," which involves recognizing the *mem* as
enclitic or perhaps adverbial (cf. McDaniel, *Biblica* 49 [1968],
203–4). For *hōmat* read <*ni*> *hhemet* ("repentant," "remorseful";
Niphal participle fem. from *nāham*) on the supposition that the
correct text was lost under the influence of vs. 8. For a very
similar pattern in a poetic line cf. Isa 52:2: "O captive daughter
Zion," *šᵉbīyyāh bat ṣīyyōn* and Jer 46:19; 48:18 and Zech 2:11,
all with *yōšebet bat* X (place name).

relief. *Pūgat* is either a case where the feminine ending *t* has
been retained in the absolute singular, or a construct in a construction of the *śimhat baqqāṣīr* type.

19. The meaning of "Pour out your heart," which occurs only
twice in the Old Testament (here and Ps 62:8[9H]) is apparently
very much like that of the common English expression, hence the
sense is "give expression to your innermost thoughts and feelings."
Compare also I Sam 1:15. "Like water" is a stock simile used
with the verb "pour out"; cf. Deut 12:16, 24; 15:23; Ps 79:3;
Hosea 5:10.

MT adds a fourth line at the end of this verse: "Who fainted
from hunger at every street corner." In the opinion of most commentators, this is an addition, a mosaic of bits from vss. 11c,
12b, and 4:1b. The reference to "your children" in the previous
line provided the peg for the addition. It is the only one of the
four lines which can be omitted without raising new problems
within the verse.

20. *they have raised.* The *hapax legomenon ṭippūhīm* and the
related verb *ṭippahtī* in vs. 22 are translated as having to do with
child-rearing since this fits the contexts well, and is supported by
an Akkadian cognate *ṭepū* as well; cf. W. von Soden, "Zum
akkadischen Wörterbuch, 6–14," *Orientalia,* N.S. 16 (1947), 77–78.

To 20c and 21a and b, which speak of the dead in the
sanctuary and the streets, compare "Lamentation over the Destruction of Ur," ANET, p. 459: "In its lofty gates, where they were
wont to promenade, dead bodies were lying about; / In its boule-
vards, where the feasts were celebrated, *scattered they lay.* / In all
its streets, where they were wont to promenade, dead bodies were

lying about; / In its places, where the festivities of the land took place, the people lay in heaps."

22. *men to attack me from all sides.* Whatever the correct rendering of Jeremiah's *māgōr missābīb* in each of its occurrences (Jer 6:25; 20:3, 10; 46:5; 49:29; also Ps 31:13[14H]), and whatever its relation to the present passage may be, it seems best not to translate *megūray missābīb* here "my terrors on every side" (so RSV and similarly many others), since it seems that men are referred to—to have "terrors" invited to a festival would involve a mixture of metaphors not typical of Hebrew poetry. "Attackers" is suggested by the context and by the meaning of *gūr* in several biblical passages (see KB³, s.v. *gūr* II and especially Job 18:19) and also perhaps by Ugar. *gr* in CTA 14 (=Krt) 110–111: *wgr.nn.'rm.* Or one might propose a meaning "Those who lie in wait for/besiege me," based on *gūr* I, "to abide"; note that in Ps 59:3[4H] the parallel to *yāgūrū 'ālay* is *'ārebū lenapšī.* The pointing of MT is probably incorrect, but the correct vocalization is uncertain; perhaps best is *megōray,* as a contracted form of an assumed Polel participle **megōreray* (cf. GKC, para. 72cc). Rudolph also points thus but translates: "those who terrify me," which gives good sense. For a fuller discussion, on which this NOTE has drawn, see McDaniel, *Biblica* 49 (1969), 42–44.

COMMENT

In externals the second Lamentation is very much like the first. It is an alphabetic acrostic poem of three-line stanzas, and only the first line of each stanza is made to conform to the acrostic pattern. The only formal difference is that, contrary to the normal order of the Hebrew alphabet, *pe* precedes *ayin* (as also in chapters 3 and 4). The reason for this variation escapes us. The meter is predominantly *"Qinah"* meter (see the Introduction). The date seems to be the same as that for chapter 1: shortly after the fall of Jerusalem in 587 B.C.

In other respects, however, chapter 2 contrasts with chapter 1. Here there is less of the personification of Zion, and only at the very end (vss. 20–22) does she speak for herself. For the most part it is the poet who speaks of what happened to Zion, or who addresses the city. Moreover, the structure of the chapter is determined not so much by a psychological progression, as was true of the first poem, but primarily by a logical sequence of material. Though this order is not strictly kept to in every detail, in general this second poem may be outlined as follows:

Outline

A. Since it is Yahweh who destroyed Zion . . .
    1. Yahweh himself destroyed Zion, vss. 1–9a
    2. How and why Yahweh destroyed Zion, vss. 9b–17
        a) The destruction and its cause described by the poet, vss. 9b–12
        b) The poet continues, but addresses Zion directly, vss. 13–16
        c) The theme restated: Yahweh has destroyed Zion, vs. 17
B. Therefore cry out to Yahweh! vss. 18–19
C. Zion's anguished appeal, vss. 20–22

The main point of this chapter is that it was Yahweh himself who destroyed city and people, and the writer seldom strays very far from this idea. Even when Zion herself finally appears and appeals to God, her words are not so much a prayer for help as a helpless restatement of the principal theme. The agent of destruction, the Lord (or Yahweh, cf. NOTE on 1:14) is introduced in the very first line and the name is given unusual prominence by the word-order of the Hebrew: it is separated from the verb and placed first in the second colon. The exact sense of line 1 is unfortunately uncertain (see NOTE), but the following lines express clear and vivid ideas. The extent of the catastrophe is described as a fall from the sky—traditional in Hebrew as the absolute height—to earth, the absolute depth (cf. Prov 25:3: "The sky for height and the earth for depth . . . ," and many other passages). Weiser sees here an allusion to the mythological motif of a fall from heaven (Isa 14:12; Ezek 28:17), but that is perhaps over-specific. Next it is the mystery of the divine wrath which is brought into prominence: Yahweh paid no attention to the fact that Zion was his own "footstool," his own elect city and temple, sign of his presence with his people. This paradox is restated, directly and indirectly, throughout the chapter. This was a "day of the Lord's anger" (cf. COMMENT on 1:12) which struck his own people.

In succeeding verses (2–5) God is depicted as a mighty warrior, pitiless in his anger. He has struck both the buildings (2a, b; 5a, b) and the people of Zion. Her king and princes, who were sacred persons because of special closeness to him, he has brought low and defiled (2c). Three familiar metaphors follow: Yahweh has "lopped off Israel's horns," that is, has destroyed her strength and pride (see NOTE); he has turned back his (Israel's; see NOTE) "right hand," a frequent symbol of prowess (often of God, but also, as here, of men, e.g. Ps 137:5); and his anger burned like fire against Jacob.

The following verse (4) makes the picture of God as a warrior still more explicit. On the history of this conception of God, see P. Miller, "God the Warrior," *Interpretation* 19 (1965), 39–46; F. M. Cross, Jr., "The Divine Warrior in Israel's Early Cult," in *Biblical Motifs: Origins and Transformations,* ed. Alexander Altmann (Cambridge, Mass., 1966), pp. 11–30. With bow and sword (?—see NOTE), he killed all the fine-looking warriors of Israel. The tendency in Israelite thought to ignore secondary causes and think of Yahweh as the cause of all calamity (cf. Amos 3:6) could not appear more unmistakably! After a reiteration of the statement that Yahweh destroyed the city's fortifications, there is a brief allusion to the people's reaction: moaning and mourning were abundant ("moaning and mourning" is an attempt to reflect the obviously intentional assonance of the Heb. *ta'ᵃnīyyāh wā'ᵃnīyyāh,* derivatives of the same root; this pair is found also in Isa 29:2).

In verses 6 and 7 the dominant idea is that touched on already in vs. 1: Yahweh has destroyed what was sacred to himself, both sacred objects (altar, sanctuary, temple), people (king and priest), and institutions (festival and sabbath). The enemy was allowed to raise an unholy din in the temple, so that it sounded as though a kind of witches' sabbath were being celebrated.

Lest there be any misconception, it is made clear that Yahweh did all this, not through inadvertence, but deliberately; he planned it (8); he stretched out the line, the deliberate act of a man planning a project (see NOTE); and he did not change his mind. Mention of the walls and ramparts constitutes a bridge to the next stanza. Rather often the author deliberately "syncopates," that is he sees to it that divisions of thought and formal divisions do not always coincide (cf. e.g. vss. 11–12; 3:12–13 and the beginning of COMMENT on chapter 3). "Her gates have sunk into the earth," is probably meant as a literal statement to which may be compared "The Curse of Agade," ANET, p. 649, line 167: "In the gates of the land the doors stood deep in dust." If not, one might suppose that the "gates" are personified here, like the "mourning" walls of the preceding line (cf. 1:4), and then "sunk into the earth" would recall what is said elsewhere of persons; to have one's feet sink (*ṭāba'*) into mud (Ps 69:2, 14[3, 15H]; Jer 38:22) is a figure for being in great distress.

With the next line (9b) the attention shifts for a time away from Yahweh and toward the city herself, especially the people. All the most important people are either gone or not functioning: king, princes, priests—it is they who would normally have supplied the "instruction" (*tōrāh*)—and prophets. (Cf. Ezek 7:26; Micah 3:6; Ps 74:9; I Sam 3:1.) The elders mourn for Zion with typical mourning rites, as though for a dead person. (On the whole passage, see Hedwig Jahnow, *Das hebräische Leichenlied im Rahmen der Völkerdichtung,* BZAW 36 [Giessen, 1923], p. 7.) They sit on the ground. This traditional attitude (cf. Ezek 26:16;

Job 2:12; II Sam 13:31; Josh 7:6) expresses humiliation, the
earth being symbolic of lowness. In this pose also a man was
in direct contact with dirt, a recurring image for mortality. If
the verb *dāmam* is correctly translated here (see NOTE), the elders
keep silence for a period, another customary mourning observance,
on which see N. Lohfink, "Enthielten die im Alten Testament
bezeugten Klageriten eine Phase des Schweigens?" VT 12 (1962),
260–77. They put dirt on their heads, an age-old mourning gesture
attested already in Ugaritic texts (from about the fifteenth century
B.C.). This was an acting-out of "Dust thou art and unto dust
shalt thou return." For parallels see Josh 7:6; I Sam 4:12; II Sam
1:2; 15:32; Ezek 27:30; Job 2:12; 42:6; Neh 9:1. El performs
this rite in a Ugaritic myth (CTA 5=UT 67 vi 14–16); for an
Akkadian parallel see CAD, s.v. *eperu,* p. 187. They put on
sackcloth. The virgins let their heads sink to the earth. The specific
mention of "old men" and "young women" ("virgins") as the
two classes that mourn is perhaps to be accounted for as a merism,
that is, these are the two opposite limits of the population, and
the sense is: the whole people mourns. On the other hand, as
maintained above (on 1:4), mention of "virgins" in such a context
may derive from an old literary tradition, the source of which is
the myth of the mourning Virgin goddess.

In vs. 11, the poet speaks of his own consuming grief. As
frequently in the Old Testament, the bowels are thought of as the
physical organ involved in intense emotion. The "pouring out" of
the liver is not elsewhere mentioned in the MT as it stands, but
Ps 7:5[6H] is probably to be read "He sets my liver (not
kᵉbōdî, "my honor") in the dirt," which would be a close parallel
to the present verse.

The famine which struck the little children especially is depicted
in a dramatic vignette. Starving children ask their mothers for
bread and wine, but there is none, and they faint in the streets,
or expire in their mothers' laps.

The description of Zion's misery continues, but takes a new
turn as the poet for a time addresses the city directly (vss. 13–16).
This prepares the way for the imperatives addressed to Zion in
the next major section, beginning vs. 18. The questions of vs. 13
are rhetorical, for there is no adequate comparison for the present
wretchedness of Zion. (It is not clear just why finding a comparison
for Zion would *comfort* her; one explanation [Jahnow, Rudolph]

is that a person will feel better if he is shown that his case is not unique, but this is rather unconvincing.) Even when the author goes on to use a simile—"vast as the sea"—this is actually another way of saying the same thing, since the sea is the element traditional for expressing size and length. Already in a Ugaritic text (CTA 23=UT 52 33–35) El's "hand" is "long as the sea" (cf. Jean Nougayrol, *Ugaritica*, V [Paris, 1969], text 3, RS 24 245, line 2). According to Job 11:9, no one can take the measure of God: ". . . its breadth is greater than the sea" (cf. Isa 48:18; Ps 104:25). If a thing is beyond the sea, it is as unreachable as something in the sky (Deut 30:12–13). Zion is shattered totally, beyond repair.

From speaking of Jerusalem's present misery, the writer turns for a single stanza (vs. 14) to consideration of its cause. The people had sinned, but the prophets, those who supposedly had the most spiritual and moral insight, did not lay it bare but painted it over with oracles of "Peace, peace." (See NOTE on "whitewash.") Israel's destruction was not inevitable. Had her sin been made open and had she repented (the idea is implicit, not expressed in the terse poetic line), she might have enjoyed good times again. (On this meaning of Heb. *šūb šĕbūt* cf. e.g. Deut 30:3; Ezek 16:53; Hosea 6:11; Amos 9:14.)

After this single backward look the poem returns to the present misery, which is depicted under a familiar figure. All those who pass by Jerusalem express their contempt of her in her ruinous state. (Cf. I Kings 9:8; Jer 18:16; 19:8; 49:17; 50:13; Ezek 5:14; 36:34; Zeph 2:15; Ps 80:12[13H].) Her proud title "perfection of beauty," hers by right of being Yahweh's chosen city, is now flung in her teeth. This is reminiscent of the lines from Ps 42:3, 10[4, 11H]: "My foes revile me, saying to me, 'Where is your God?'" Adding to the intolerable nature of what the enemies say is the fact that they are, even if unconscious of it, doing God's work. The following verse (17) makes this explicit, but it is there already in the language of the enemies. Their "We have consumed" echoes "The Lord consumed" of vss. 2 and 5; their "day" recalls "the day of his wrath," vs. 1.

The first main section of the lament closes with a return to the major theme with which the poem began: Yahweh has done what he planned. With a certain hyperbole it is even asserted that Israel's destruction was his purpose from "olden times."

The call for Zion to pray heaps up expressive devices to make it clear that her appeal to God must be both sincere and extraordinary. She is to cry "from the heart" (see NOTE at vs. 18) and to "pour out her heart," (vs. 19) shedding tears continually, night and day. The last phrase "for the lives of your children" leads into the prayer itself, which is about "children" in two senses. In the first place, the slaughtered citizens of Jerusalem are thought of as the children of the personified Zion, who weeps over them like Rachel. In a more literal sense, it is the actual little children who are uppermost in the poet's mind; they are mentioned first and last.

Zion's prayer does not contain any explicit petition, only that Yahweh should look on: "Consider whom you have treated so." This comes close to being a reproach to Yahweh, or if not that, then at least a strong appeal to his compassion. Granted that Jerusalem had sinned, the actual conquest brought ghastly extremes of suffering which seemed to those involved out of proportion to any guilt of the sufferers. This appears most clearly in the case of the children and the mothers, who suffered not only starvation but loss of all humanity. References to cannibalism in time of siege frequently appear in the Old Testament and other ancient Near Eastern literature; see COMMENT on 1:11. Also revolting to ordinary human religious feeling is the idea that men of God should be killed right in the sanctuary where they ministered (20c). In the lines rendered *"Should* woman eat . . . Should priest and prophet . . ."* the imperfect verbs could also be rendered as incredulous questions: "Can it be that women eat?" etc.

None has escaped. Old men and boys, young men and women, they lie in the streets, unburied. As in vs. 17, the poet puts Yahweh, the ultimate and in his mind real cause, in the foreground; only at the very end (22c) do the human enemies receive notice. The combination of words "the day of your wrath" and "slaughtered," *ṭābaḥtā,* with "as to a festival," *mōʿēd,* suggests that the writer is alluding to the picture elaborated most fully in Isa 34: the day of God's wrath is a grisly banquet, at which men are slaughtered like animals of sacrifice. Note that vocabulary similar to that of vs. 21 recurs in Ps 44:22[23H] and Jer 12:3, where the comparison to sacrificial animals is explicit.

The human agents of Yahweh's wrath are brought into the picture at the very end. Yahweh invited them to gather on all sides of the city and lay siege to it. Since they encircled it, there was no chance for escape (cf. Jer 50:29 "Encamp against her on all sides; let no one get away"). Like the first poem, so this also ends on a low, pathetic tone, as mother Zion mourns once again the loss of her children.

III
EVERYMAN
(3:1–66)

Aleph	1 "I am the man who has been through trouble under the rod of his anger.
Aleph	2 He led and guided me—into darkness, not light,
Aleph	3 He turned his hand against me above all, again and again, all day.
Beth	4 He wore out my flesh and skin; he broke my bones.
Beth	5 He besieged and encircled me with poverty and hardship.
Beth	6 He made me sit in the dark like those long dead.
Gimel	7 He shut me in so I cannot escape; he put me in heavy chains.
Gimel	8 Even when I cry out and ask for help, he shuts out my prayer.
Gimel	9 He has blocked up my ways with cut stones; he has made my paths crooked.
Daleth	10 He is a lurking bear to me, a lion in hiding:
Daleth	11 He turned me aside and tore me apart. He made me desolate.
Daleth	12 He bent his bow and set me up as a target for his arrows.
He	13 He shot me in the vitals with shafts from his quiver.

He   14 I have become a joke to all my people; all day long they mock me in song.

He   15 He gave me my fill of bitter things; he sated me with wormwood.

Waw   16 He ground my teeth in the gravel; he trampled me into the dust.

Waw   17 I despaired of having peace; I forgot everything good.

Waw   18 I thought, 'My lasting hope in Yahweh has perished.'

Zayin   19 I remember my miserable wandering, the wormwood and poison.

Zayin   20 Within myself I surely remember, and am despondent.

Zayin   21 Yet one thing I will keep in mind which will give me hope:

Heth   22 Yahweh's mercy is surely not at an end, nor is his pity exhausted.

Heth   23 It is new every morning. Great is your faithfulness!

Heth   24 Yahweh is my portion, I tell myself, therefore I will hope.

Teth   25 Yahweh is good to the person who waits for him, to the man who seeks him.

Teth   26 It is good that a man hope in quiet for Yahweh's deliverance.

Teth   27 It is good for a man that he bear the yoke in his youth.

Yod   28 Let him sit in silence by himself when it is heavy on him.

Yod   29 Let him put his mouth in the dirt — maybe there is hope.

Yod	30 Let him turn his cheek to the one who strikes him; let him have his fill of disgrace.
Kaph	31 Because the Lord does not reject forever . . . ;
Kaph	32 Because after he has afflicted he will have pity, out of his abounding mercy;
Kaph	33 Because he does not deliberately torment men, or afflict them
Lamed	34 By crushing under foot all the prisoners of the earth,
Lamed	35 By denying a man justice before the Most High,
Lamed	36 By twisting a man's case without the Lord seeing.
Mem	37 Who was it who 'spoke and it was done?' It was the Lord who gave the command.
Mem	38 Both bad and good take place at the command of the Most High.
Mem	39 Why should a man complain over his sins, as long as he is still alive?
Nun	40 Let us rather test and examine our ways, and return to Yahweh.
Nun	41 Let us lift our heart along with our hands to God above."
Nun	42 "We have rebelled and disobeyed. You have not forgiven.
Samekh	43 You have enveloped us in anger and pursued us; you have slain without sparing.
Samekh	44 You have wrapped yourself in cloud so no prayer could get through.
Samekh	45 You make us a despised off-scouring among the nations.

Pe	46 All our enemies open their mouths wide at us.
Pe	47 We have been through panic and pit, wreck and ruin."
Pe	48 "My eyes run with streams of tears at the ruin of my people.
Ayin	49 My eyes will stream without stopping, without relief,
Ayin	50 Until Yahweh looks out from above to see.
Ayin	51 The affliction done to me, has consumed my eyes."
Sade	52 "Those who are my enemies for no reason hunted me like a bird.
Sade	53 They shut me tight in a pit and threw stones at me.
Sade	54 Waters came over my head. I said, 'I am cut off.'
Qof	55 Out of the lowest pit, Yahweh, I call your name.
Qof	56 Hear my voice — Do not close your ears — to relieve me, to save me!
Qof	57 Be near when I call you; tell me not to be afraid.
Resh	58 Lord, be on my side in this struggle; redeem my life.
Resh	59 Yahweh, see the injustice I suffer; uphold my cause.
Resh	60 See how they took revenge on me, plotted against me.
Shin	61 Listen to how they reproach me, Yahweh, how they plot against me.
Shin	62 The speech and the thoughts of my enemies are against me all day.

Shin	63 Look, in everything they do I am the butt of their mockery.
Taw	64 Give them back, Yahweh, what they have coming, for what their hands have done.
Taw	65 Give them anguish of heart, as your curse on them!
Taw	66 May you pursue them in anger and wipe them out from under Yahweh's heaven!"

3:2. This is one of the lines where the first colon contains two verbs, joined by *waw*-consecutive (see NOTE on 1:6 above). The second colon typically (not always) contains elements which modify *both* the verbs. Hence the effect is to separate sharply between the verbal predicates and the following modifiers; the caesura seems to be emphasized. Begrich, ZS 9 (1933–34), 174–75, lists similar examples mostly in the Psalms (most of his, however, do not involve a *waw*-consecutive form). He accounts for the construction as due to the necessity to fill up the line when it consisted of a single sentence, but that seems not to have been the only motive.

3. *turned his hand against me.* A. Fitzgerald has quite correctly observed that the verb *hāpak* is not elsewhere combined with *yād*, "hand," except in cases where turning of a chariot is spoken of, which obviously does not apply to the present case; hence he would understand the text quite differently, "He reverses his love all the day"; see "Hebrew *yd*='Love' and 'Beloved,'" CBQ 29 (1967), 368–69. In the present writer's opinion, the Hebrew phrase he would substitute is just as unparalleled as the MT (since Ps 105:25, which he cites, is not a good parallel), and his interpretation more forced than the traditional understanding of the Hebrew text.

5. *poverty.* Reading (as also JPS) *rē'š* (=*rēš*, cf. Prov 6:11; 30:8) for MT *rō'š*, "poison." The combination of concrete and abstract in MT "venom and hardship" seems unacceptable.

11. *tore me apart.* Since the Heb. *waypašš^eḥēnī* occurs only here, and the translation relies on the Syriac and the Targum, it is not certain that the image of God as a predatory animal continues into this verse especially since *d^erākay sōrēr* is also of uncertain meaning.

13. *in the vitals.* Literally "in my kidneys," as the most vulnerable and sensitive target; cf. Job 16:13.

14. A *Sebir,* or ancient conjecture by Jewish textual scholars, gives "all *peoples*" instead of "all my people," and this plural turns up elsewhere in the textual tradition. It seems to arise from a desire to interpret the poem as referring to the whole people, which MT makes difficult at this point.

17. *I despaired,* etc. Following the suggestion of Horace Hummel, "Enclitic *Mem* in Early Northwest Semitic, Especially in Hebrew," *Journal of Biblical Literature* 76 (1957), 105, who recognizes in the initial *m* of *miššālōm* an enclitic *mem* which should be attached to the preceding verb. *šālōm* then becomes the direct object of *zānaḥ,* which is usually transitive.

18. *lasting hope.* Hebrew "my enduring and my hope" is taken to be a hendiadys.

19. *I remember.* The imperative of MT (*zᵉkōr*) has seemed difficult to many commentators in this context, because the change in the speaker's attitude seems to begin only later, at 21. Some have preferred to read here a noun, *zēker,* or to take MT not as an imperative but as the infinitive *zᵉkōr,* yielding a translation, "The memory of my miserable wandering is wormwood," etc. The present translation is based on context and the reading of LXX, which gives a first-person form "I remember." Since the Greek translator does not ordinarily depart from the text before him in such matters, it is best to assume that his Hebrew text had either *zākartī* or possibly *zākōr ʾᵃnī,* infinitive absolute followed by independent personal pronoun indicating the subject. Interpretation of this line is to some extent tied up with the question of how one reads vs. 20; see the NOTE following.

my miserable wandering. Cf. NOTE on *mᵉrūdehā* at 1:7.

20. *am despondent.* Reading the Qre *wᵉtāšōaḥ,* from the root *šḥḥ.* For close parallels, see Pss 42:5, 6, 11[6, 7, 12H]; 43:5. (Ktib implies *tāšīaḥ,* evidently a Hiphil of *šwḥ;* this is unparalleled and it is not clear what sense the form would have.) The tradition that MT at this point embodies a *Tiqqun Sopherim* raises a minor problem concerning this otherwise unproblematic line, but the difficulty has been exacerbated by confusion on the part of commentators. The *Tiqqune Sopherim* ("corrections of the scribes") are changes made in the Hebrew text at an early stage, deliberately, for dogmatic reasons. These slight emendations were intended to eliminate expressions which were thought to be too anthropomorphic, or otherwise inconsistent with the dignity of God. Where tradi-

tion records that the scribes deliberately changed the text, there is, of course, a strong presumption that the existing MT is wrong. In the case here, however, such a conclusion may not necessarily be correct. (a) This verse is not given in the most ancient lists as containing a *Tiqqun,* and when it does appear, in a longer list (Tanchuma at Exod 15:7), there is no indication what the original reading was. (b) The idea that the original reading was *napšekā,* "your soul," seems to go back, as far as I have been able to discover, to Abraham Geiger, *Urschrift und Übersetzungen der Bibel* (Breslau, 1857), p. 315; note, however, that Geiger does not state clearly whether he has a Masoretic list giving *napšekā* as the original or whether he is only assuming that this was the original. That the original was *napšekā* is also assumed in the lengthy discussion of this verse by C. D. Ginsburg, *Introduction to the Masoretico-Critical Edition of the Hebrew Bible* (London, 1897), p. 361. Yet, surprisingly, a Masoretic list of fifteen (*sic;* the standard number is eighteen) *Tiqqune Sopherim* which Ginsburg prints in a footnote on p. 351 and which he calls "prior to the Masoretic recension when the number was already fixed" reads as follows: *npšw hyh ktwb,* "the original reading was *napšō, his* soul"! (c) In this same connection Ginsburg refers to other lists which he had previously printed in his four-volume *The Massorah* (London, 1880–1905), letter *Taw,* para. 206, Vol. II, 710—but at this point the *Tiqqun* is said to concern, not the word *nepeš* and its suffix, but the preposition; *'ālekā,* "upon you," is supposed to have been the original, altered to *'ālay.*

To sum up, one may doubt that the Masoretes had any ancient tradition as to the original reading in this case. If the text has in fact been altered at some point, the change is far from obvious, for none of the conjectures advanced as to the "original" reading are convincingly grammatical and idiomatic, whereas MT Qre has strong support from the parallels cited, Pss 42:5, 6, 11[6, 7, 12H]; 43:5, and (disregarding the Ktib/Qre complications) is supported by the versions as well. On the *Tiqqune Sopherim* in general, see Saul Lieberman, *Hellenism in Jewish Palestine* (New York, 1950), pp. 28–37.

22. *is surely not at an end.* Reading with many commentators *tammū* for MT *tām^enū.* The Targum implies *tammū* as the reading of its *Vorlage* and the Syriac may, though Albrektson questions the latter point. The two *kī's* are asseverative, not causal; "surely" is

intended to reflect their force. On this particle see references in McDaniel, *Biblica* 49 (1968), 210, n. 2. McDaniel's interpretation of the verse is noteworthy (pp. 212–14). He vocalizes *kī lō' timmānū kī lō' kīlū* etc. and translates "The mercies of Yahweh are innumerable! Verily, his compassions are immeasurable," but the attempt to defend MT is perhaps more ingenious than convincing.

25. *the person.* MT consonantal text *qww* seems to stand for a singular (**qōwēw* from **qōwēhū*); the vocalization suggests a plural. The parallel word *nepeš* is singular and favors the singular reading, though this is scarcely conclusive evidence.

26. The MT of the first colon is slightly corrupt, and cannot be explained as it stands. There is widespread agreement that the sense of the line must be approximately that given here, and that the roots *yḥl,* "wait," and *dūm/dāmam,* "be silent," must have stood in the original in some form. Albrektson, pp. 146–48, has a thorough discussion of previous suggestions. The present translation presupposes loss of a *kī* (by similarity of *k* to final *b* of *ṭōb?*) and several lesser errors; original perhaps *ṭōb <kī> yōḥīl dūmām.*

27. Some Hebrew MSS and some Greek MSS and the Vulgate have *"from* his youth." Since this is a much more common expression in the Old Testament than *"in* (his, etc.) youth," it seems preferable to retain MT here, as the less common expression.

28. *is heavy.* The rare verb *nāṭal* otherwise means "to lift, bear" in the Old Testament, but the related noun *nēṭel* means "weight" in Prov 27:3 (parallel to *kōbed*), and the verb *nṭal* in Syriac means "to be heavy." For *nāṭal 'al* cf. *kābēd 'al.* This proposal eliminates the need to press *nāṭal* here to mean "he (Yahweh) lifted up *and laid on"* as is usually done.

31. The text is too short, something having been omitted in the course of its transmission, but it is impossible to supply the deficiency with anything approaching certainty or probability. "His servants" (Lowth) and "mankind" (Rudolph) have been proposed as objects.

34. To fit the acrostic the poet makes each line begin with an infinitive preceded by *l.* By itself this Hebrew construction does not make a sentence, and the infinitives must depend on some finite verb. Many commentators and translators have construed the infinitives as objects of *'ᵃdōnāy lō' rā'āh* in 36, which is translated either as a question ("When one crushes under foot . . . did not the Lord see it?") or a statement ("To crush, . . . the Lord does not

approve," RSV; cf. Rudolph's "When one crushes, . . . the Lord does not mind it!"). But this requires the assumption that the word-order is odd, with the series of infinitives *preceding* the verbs on which they depend. Moreover, the Hebrew would be odd even if *lō' rā'āh* preceded, since *rā'āh* is not normally (actually, in no case that the present writer could discover; Budde makes the same observation) followed by an infinitive with *l*. Hence it seems preferable to explain the infinitives as dependent on the parallel verbs in the preceding verse (vs. 33: *lō' 'innāh . . . wayyaggeh*). *'ᵃdōnāy lō' rā'āh* is then understood to be a circumstantial clause, cf. GKC, para. 156, d–g. On the meaning of the verse, see the COMMENT. In any explanation, it remains a bit odd that names of God are used in the infinitive phrases of 35 and 36 rather than pronouns as here in 34 ("under foot," literally "under his feet"), but one may compare similar phenomena in 2:20, 22 and especially vs. 66 below: "May you (Yahweh is being addressed) pursue them in anger and wipe them out from under Yahweh's heaven!" Cf. also e.g. Amos 4:11: "I (Yahweh) overthrew some of you as when God overthrew Sodom and Gomorrah."

37. Since in this and the following verse it is obvious that the poet means to assert positively that God *does* command both good and bad, one must look on the *lō'* in each line as either: (a) a negative, "not," and read the lines as rhetorical questions, or (b) asseverative or emphatic *lamed*'s. This explanation is preferred by McDaniel, *Biblica* 49 (1968), 206–8, where a bibliography on emphatic *lamed* is given. The latter alternative has been adopted here, but the difference in sense is slight, whichever is chosen.

39. The MT has often been regarded as corrupt, but it seems defensible (Meek, Weiser, Kraus, and Albrektson retain it), though the Hebrew is rather odd. A literal rendering would be: "Why should a living man (*'ādām ḥay*) complain, a man (*geber*) over his sins." The phrase *'ādām ḥay* may be intended to suggest the idea "Where there's life there's hope" (cf. the *keleb ḥay* of Eccles 9:4) and its converse in Israelite thought, that the dead have no hope. The parallelism seems to involve ellipsis from the second colon of the verb and interrogative, which must be supplied from the first colon.

40. *test. ḥāpaś* more frequently means "search for" but the idea here is not of trying to find the right path, but of examination of

one's conduct; the parallel verb *ḥāqar* is often used so, and *ḥāpaś* has the sense "test" also in Prov 20:27.

41. *'el* is used for *'al,* as often. The sense is "with, along with," and it may deserve notice that this use of *'al* is especially common in prescriptions for sacrifice: X is to be sacrificed with (*'al*) Y; see BDB, s.v. *'al* 4c.

43. The verb *sakkōtāh* is probably not reflexive, since elsewhere the Qal is always transitive. Hence not "you covered yourself," but "you covered *us*" the object-pronoun on *wattirdᵉpēnū* serving for both verbs; cf. vss. 2, 5 and 66 for similar shared objects. Note also that there is no objection to interpreting this first *sakkōtāh* (here) as a bit different in its syntactic function from the identical form in the next line; cf. the successive *pnē*'s in 4:16a and 16b.

51. *The affliction done to me . . . eyes.* MT is corrupt and yields no acceptable sense, as recognized by most. Very literally rendered, MT is: "My eye has done to my soul from (or, more than) all the daughters of my people." Read perhaps *'ōnī 'ōlal lᵉnapšī mᵉkall<eh>bᵉnōt 'ēnay.* For another case where *'ōnī* has been confused with *'ēnī,* see II Sam 16:12. On *bᵉnōt 'ēnay* cf. Lam 2:18 *bat 'ayin.* To the whole verse compare Ps 69:3[4H]: "I am worn out from calling, my throat is parched, my eyes are consumed" (*kālū 'ēnay*).

56. *Šāma'tā* is interpreted here as a precative perfect; see NOTE on 1:21. In 55–66 these perfects are interspersed with imperative or other volitive forms, and note also the confirmation of this interpretation from Ps 130:1, a closely parallel passage: "From the depths I call you" (*qᵉrā'tīkā*) parallels vs. 55: "Out of the lowest pit, Yahweh, I call (*qārā'tī*) your name," and Ps 130:2 "Lord hear (*šim'āh,* an imperative) my voice" parallels vs. 56 *qōlī šāma'tā* (perfect), which must then be: "Hear my voice." Also interpreted as precative perfects in this passage are vs. 57: *qārabtā* and *'āmartā;* vs. 58: *rabtā* and *gā'altā;* vs. 59: *rā'ītāh;* vs. 60: *rā'ītāh;* vs. 61: *šāma'tā.*

The latter part of this verse is difficult grammatically and metrically (it is hard to find a satisfactory division into two parts), but for lack of a convincing improvement MT has been retained and translated rather literally. The only change is of *lᵉšaw'ātī* ("to my cry") to *līšū'ātī* ("for my salvation, to save me"). The latter reading is supported by LXX, Symmachus, and perhaps Syriac, and fits better with *lᵉrawḥātī* ("for my relief, to relieve me"). *lᵉrawḥātī* is odd after "Do not close your ears," where we expect as object (following *l*) either a person or a word meaning "cry, voice" or the like. Yet its aptness in this context is suggested by *qrw lh b'q' w'nn brwḥ' ln,* "they *called on* him (cf. vs. 55) in distress and he answered them with *relief* for them." These lines from a Palmyrene Aramaic inscription, published by Dja'far al-Hassani and Jean Starcky, "Autels palmyréniens découverts près de la source Efca," *Annales archéologiques de la Syrie* 3 (1953), 160–63, are paralleled in another Palmyrene inscription published by Jean-Baptiste Chabot, *Corpus Inscriptionum Semiticarum,* Pars secunda, Tomus tertius, Fasciculus primus (Paris, 1926), no. 4100. Chabot called attention to the biblical parallel, Ps 118:5, especially close when the Syriac and Targum of the verse are considered. These parallels (and more remote, Pss 18:20; 31:9) caution against deletion of *lᵉrawḥātī*. Some (e.g. Rudolph) have deleted *lᵉšaw'ātī*, and indeed it looks suspiciously like a double reading, but deletion would leave a very short colon.

63. *in everything they do.* Literally "(In) their sitting down and rising up." The combination of "sit" and "rise" is a familiar meristic idiom in Hebrew for the whole round of a person's daily activities; cf. e.g. Deut 6:7. The suffix *-ām* on each of the nouns is here construed as the possessive suffix "their." McDaniel, *Biblica* 49 (1968), 204–5, takes it as an adverbial suffix (cf. first NOTE on 2:18), and reinterprets other elements in the verse as well. But one may question whether sufficient evidence has up to now been advanced for free use of adverbial *-ām,* apart from the few stereotyped adverbs where it has long been recognized. In other respects also, MT seems defensible as it stands, despite unusual word-order.

65. *anguish of heart.* Heb. *mᵉginnat lēb* is of uncertain meaning. This rendering, which is also that of JPS, at least fits the context. RSV "dullness of heart" is preferred by many commentators, who associate the word with a root *gnn,* "cover," but this seems too weak for the context. Rudolph and Kraus suggest "delusion, confusion," which also fits reasonably well, but is scarcely established by the etymology supplied (Ar. *jinn, majnūn*).

66. *pursue them.* The object "them" is supplied from the following verb ("and wipe them out"). G. R. Driver was the first to point out that in cases of parallel words only one needs an explicit pronominal suffix in Hebrew poetic style; he cited this passage as an example; see "Hebrew Studies," *Journal of the Royal Asiatic Society,* 1948, pp. 164–65. Cf. now Dahood, *Psalms III, 100–150* (1970), pp. 431–32.

COMMENT

Chapter 3 stands apart from the other chapters of the book in both form and content. Formally, it is an alphabetic acrostic poem, like 1, 2, and 4, and as in 1 and 2, the stanzas each have three lines. The acrostic is of a more demanding type, however, since the initial word of each of the three lines is made to fit the acrostic pattern. Thus there are three *aleph* lines, three *beth* lines, and so on. This elaborateness is surpassed only in Ps 119. In addition, the author is fond of repeating the initial word or particle, thus *gādar* in 7 and 9; *ṭōb* in 25–27; *kī* in 31–33; *sakkōtāh* in 43, 44; *'ēnī* in 49 and 51 (if the text is correct), and *rā'ītāh* in 59 and 60. He also repeats forms that are not completely identical, but from the same root: *dᵉrākay* (11) and *dārak; zᵉkōr* (19; vocalization somewhat uncertain) and *zākōr* (20). A counter-rhythm to the strict march of the acrostic pattern is provided by the sequence of thought, for very often breaks in the thought occur *within* the stanzas, and correspondingly, ideas are conjoined across the stanzas as divided by the acrostic. Thus in sense 3 goes with 4 (see COMMENT); 6 with 7; 12 with 13; 18 with 19–20; 21 with 22 ff.; 42 with 43–47; 48 with 49–51; and 60 with 61–63.

In content chapter 3 differs from the others in that there is very little specific reference to the fall of Jerusalem or the sufferings that followed. The poem begins, "I am the man who has been through trouble," and continues for a long time to speak of how this man has suffered. Thus one of the major questions that arises is: how is this chapter connected with the rest of the book? Another is: who is this man? These questions are complicated by the presence of other voices within the poem: "we" is used in vss. 40–47, and though the first singular pronoun "I" returns at vss. 48–51 and 52–66, one is led to ask whether this "I" is the same as the "I" who speaks in the first part of the poem.

The tradition that Jeremiah was the author of Lamentations had a ready-made answer for the major questions posed by the chapter: Jeremiah is the man, and he speaks of his own sufferings. The other voices that are heard in the poem are readily explained as responding to his words. When one abandons the idea of authorship by Jeremiah, however, some other explanation must be found for the "man" of vs. 1. Various approaches to an answer are summarized below; the reader should keep in mind that for all the variety of opinion represented there are often considerable areas of agreement between one scholar and another—the various approaches are not always mutually exclusive alternatives.

A favorite line of interpretation has been to see the "I" who speaks in the poem as collective. This view has been held, for example, by R. Smend, Ehrlich, Eissfeldt (*Einleitung in das Alte Testament*[3] [Tübingen, 1964], pp. 680–81), Gottwald, and Albrektson. It is Zion who speaks, Zion represented as an individual, as in chapters 1 and 2. Also Giuseppe Ricciotti, who holds to the view that Jeremiah wrote the book, comes close to this collective view because he sees Jeremiah in his suffering as identified with Jerusalem in a particularly intimate way (*Le lamentazioni di Geremia* [Turin and Rome, 1924], p. 78, note on vs. 1). This has the advantage of tying chapter 3 closely to the rest of the book, and also of accounting for the intrusion of "we" passages toward the end of the poem—the "I" and "we" are in a sense identical, since the community is speaking throughout. Yet this view, especially for vss. 1–36, encounters serious difficulties. Zion is a woman, a mother, in the other poems, whereas the speaker in chapter 3 is unmistakably male, a *geber*. The contrast is especially sharp because vs. 1 "I am the man" follows immediately on the last verses of chapter 2, with their picture of the bereaved mother Zion. Furthermore, the speaker in 3 is explicitly set apart from "my people" (*'ammī*, 14)—a point that evidently bothered ancient adherents to the collective theory as well, since the reading is changed to "peoples" (*'ammīm*) in the Syriac, some Greek manuscripts, and also in a *Sebir,* an ancient conjecture having reference to the Masoretic Text, and in some Hebrew manuscripts. In the view of the present writer, a collective theory is easier to maintain for the "I" of vss. 52–66 than for the first part of the poem, but though such a view is of considerable value in understanding the poem, it falls short of doing justice to everything in the chapter.

At the opposite end of the spectrum, there are others who have read this as a poem about an individual, for example, Bernhard Stade (*Geschichte Israels,* vol. I [Berlin, 1887], 701, n. 1) and Budde in his commentary. In the view of these scholars, the chapter has little to do with the rest of the book, and in fact was written much later. It is not concerned with the fall of Jerusalem in 587 B.C. at all. This view has the merit of acknowledging that much of the poem is about an individual's troubles, but cannot account convincingly for the presence of the "we" passages, with their references to a more than personal disaster. Moreover it seems very superficial if, having established that the chapter deals with an individual, one concludes at once that this must separate it drastically from the rest of the book. At least one ought to look for ways in which this poem, which is, if only physically and formally, central to the book, is integrated with it in thought.

Some have identified the "man" of the poem with a specific historic individual. Norman W. Porteous has argued, rather briefly, that the "man" must be King Jehoiachin ("Jerusalem-Zion: The Growth of a Symbol," in *Verbannung und Heimkehr,* Rudolph Festschrift [Tubingen, 1961], pp. 244–45). He seems not to have been followed by others in this identification, and indeed there is no specific evidence in favor of it. Rudolph, like some others before him, for example, Stade, Löhr, and Budde, identifies the "man" as the prophet Jeremiah—not that Jeremiah wrote the book, or this poem, but that the anonymous author makes Jeremiah appear so as to provide his people with an example of how faith in God triumphs over suffering. Meek also entertains this idea, but does not develop it at length. Rudolph's exegesis is illuminating, both in many individual details and in its broad explanation of the meaning of chapter 3 within the book, yet on this one point, the identification of the sufferer with Jeremiah, it is unconvincing. The description of the man's sufferings, as will be shown in detail below, is cast almost exclusively in traditional figurative language for which parallels can easily be found in the psalms of lament or in other writings of similar theme, notably Job. Hence there is nothing in the chapter that makes it necessary to think that Jeremiah, or for that matter any of the writer's contemporaries, is the one who speaks.

The view adopted here is that the sufferer of chapter 3 is indeed an individual, not a collective figure like the Zion of chapters 1 and 2. This individual is, however, not a specific historic figure, but rather the typical sufferer. He is an "Everyman," a figure who represents what any man may feel when it seems that God is against him. Through this representative sufferer the poet points the way to the nation, as he shows the man who has been through trouble moving into, then out of, near-despair to patient faith and penitence, thus becoming a model for the nation. This is the high point of the book, central to it in more than an external or formal way.

Such a line of interpretation has been taken, in major respects, by Keil and Oettli in the last century, and by others since, most recently Kraus. Rudolph's view is similar in essentials, except that he also identifies the "man" as Jeremiah, as explained above. In his commentary (p. 324), Ewald expressed the sense of the poem with particular clarity:

Then, suddenly, in the third place, an individual man appears! After all, an individual is able really to lament most deeply what he has experienced personally. The result is an expression of despair—the third, but this is the deepest. However, it is also easier for an individual to engage in deep private contemplation of the eternal relation of God to man, and thus come to a proper recognition of his own sins and the necessity of repentance, and thereby to believing prayer. Who is this individual who thus laments, reflects, and prays?—whose "I" unnoticed but at exactly the right point changes to "We"? O man, he is the image of your own self! Everyone should speak and think as he does. And so it comes about, unexpectedly, that just through this discourse which is most difficult at its beginning, for the first time pain is transformed into true prayer.

The present writer agrees with Kraus, however, that the "I" who speaks at the end (vss. 52–66) is not identical with the "I" of the beginning; at any rate, because of the preceding collective prayer in vss. 42–51, the reader is led to think that the speaker of the closing verses is praying on behalf of, or is representing, the people. The following outline summarizes the progress of thought in this rather difficult poem; details are discussed in the comments that follow.

Outline

A. An individual sufferer achieves patient faith and penitence, vss. 1–39.
  1. The sufferings a man went through, 1–16.
  2. They lead him to despair, 17–20.
  3. But he achieves hope by recalling the mercy of God, 21–38.
    a) God's mercy is abiding, 21–25.
    b) Even suffering must be good, 26–30.
    c) Because God is good and just, 31–38.
  4. A man should not complain, but repent, 39.
B. Transition: the sufferer calls on his people to return to God, vss. 40–41.
C. A common prayer of lamentation and supplication, vss. 42–66.
  1. The people speak: We have sinned and are suffering for it, 42–47.
  2. The poet's grief over his people's ruin—if only Yahweh would see! 48–51.
  3. An appeal for Yahweh to help, spoken by an individual, 52–66.

At the beginning the sufferer makes a general statement: I have been through trouble, and then he proceeds through the whole first section of the chapter (1b–16) to describe his suffering in a series of more or less isolated pictures. Most of the language is figurative rather than literal. Most of the language is also traditional, since similar things are said in psalms of lament, in Job, and elsewhere. The language and thought are for the most part clear and readily understandable without further explanation, and for this reason the specific comments that follow are mostly intended to point out parallels in other literature, and to indicate where possible the associations that link individual images. This emphasis on a rather full listing of parallels for each of the verses is also intended to substantiate the assertion made above, namely, that the "man" cannot be identified with any specific individual, as some commentators have proposed. Through vs. 9, the dominant theme might be called a reversal of the Twenty-third Psalm: the Lord is a shepherd who misleads, a ruler who oppresses and imprisons.

Or one might call it the opposite of the picture of salvation found in the Exodus and wilderness traditions and in II Isaiah; the vocabulary and imagery here are the same at numerous points, but turned to depict judgment, not grace.

"The rod of his anger" (cf. Prov 22:8 and Isa 10:5) is figurative for divine punishment, as frequently in the Old Testament, e.g. II Sam 7:14; Ps 89:32[33H]; Job 9:34; 21:9. The rod was used for chastising children, and was also carried by rulers as a symbol of their exercise of force. Shepherds also carried staves, only one of the metaphoric links between pastoral life and political life. Hence it is not inconceivable that this is the link between the "rod," šēbeṭ, of vs. 1 and the "leading" of vs. 2. Often God's leading or directing a person, or Israel (Hebrew words used are nāhag, hōlīk, hidrīk, nāḥāh, nahhēl) is explicitly compared to leading of flock or herd (Pss 77:20[21H]; 78:52–53; 80:1 [2H]; Isa 40:11; 63:13–14, etc.). In an overwhelming majority of cases the picture of divine leading is one of salvation. It is frequently part of the description of God's care for Israel in the wilderness, in the days of Moses (Exod 15:13; Pss 77:20[21H]; 78:52–53) and in the new exodus out of captivity (Isa 63: 13–14; 49:10; cf. Isa 40:11). For that reason the present verse is especially bold, and the sentence structure with its suspenseful pause after the verbs underscores the drastic reversal: "He led and guided me—into darkness, not light!" (Compare Amos 5:18.) Deliverance from darkness is also salvation imagery, associated especially often with the new exodus. While light stands for all that is positive and good, it specifically connotes freedom in some cases, just as darkness is figurative for imprisonment (cf. Isa 42: 6–7, 16; 49:9; 58:9–12; Pss 43:3; 107:10–16). This line, then, with its suggestion of a change from freedom to imprisonment, anticipates much in the following lines, especially vss. 6 and 7. (On walking in darkness, vs. 2, cf. also Isa 50:10; Ps 82:5; Eccles 2:14.) The specific phrase "turned his hand against," yahᵃpōk yādō, vs. 3, is not otherwise used of divine activity toward men, but it is obviously intended to express hostile action. By itself, the "hand" of God frequently is a name for some calamity, especially sickness; cf. Job 19:21; I Sam 5:6, etc., and the study by J. J. Roberts of the expression "hand of God" in Israelite and other ancient literature, VT 21 (1971), 244–51. This reference to God's hand thus leads naturally into vs. 4, with its reference to the flesh, skin, and bones of the sufferer. This is a recurrent motif in psalms of lament. Ps 38:2–3[3–4H] is especially close: "For your arrows have sunk into me (cf. vss. 12–13 below), and your hand has come down on me. There is no soundness in my flesh because of your indignation; there is no health in my bones because of my sin." Other close parallels, in vocabulary and thought, are Isa 38:13; Ps 32:3–4.

"Besieged" (*bānāh 'ālay*) in vs. 5 seems to involve comparison of the speaker to a city encircled by enemies; cf. Deut 20:20; II Kings 25:1; Eccles 9:14. "Encircled" (*hiqqîp 'al*) is used of towns and also, in laments, of people beset by enemies (Pss 17:9; 22:16[17H]) or by God's wrath and terrors (Ps 88:17[18H]). The last passage cited is similar to the present verse in that abstractions (here: penury and hardship) are thought of as the besiegers.

As stated above, "he made me sit in the dark" is a semifigurative expression for "He put me in prison" (Ps 107:10–16; Isa 42: 6–7; 49:9; cf. also Pss 88:6[7H]; 143:3; Micah 7:8). The prison picture is carried through into the next line and made more explicit there (vs. 7). At the same time, the picture of sitting or dwelling in darkness suggests the realm of the dead— indeed "the Dark" is a poetic term for Sheol; see Ps 88:12[13H]; Job 10:21–22; 17:13; 18:18; Eccles 6:4; 11:8. Hence the comparison follows: "like those long dead," a simile that recurs in Pss 31:12[13H]; 8:4–6[5–7H]; Isa 59:10 (in Ps 143:3 the wording is identical, but the text may have been influenced by vs. 6). The dead are forgotten and cut off from Yahweh's attention and intervention, a line of thought resumed in vs. 8.

The reference to being walled in and chained is not to be taken as an allusion to events in the life of Jeremiah, as Rudolph would have it, although the prophet did experience confinement in various ways (20:1–3; 37:21; 38:6–13; 40:1; cf. 29:26). In the first place, the surrounding lines are figurative for various sorts of distress, and one may question an exegesis which would single out just these as literally true. Secondly, this sort of image recurs in other poems. The closest parallels to the present text are Job 13:27 (repeated in 33:11): "You put my feet in the stocks, and watch over my paths." Note also Ps 88:8[9H]: "I am imprisoned, and cannot escape." Cf. also Pss 105:18; 107:10–16; 116:16;

Isa 28:22; all of which mention the bonds of prisoners, and Ps 142:7[8H]).

Even though this man of sorrows calls to God, God has shut out his prayer (vs. 8). Once again, this is a stock theme of laments. It occurs again in vs. 44, and in closely parallel form at Hab 1:2 and Job 19:7; 30:20. The most common expression used is that God "hides his face"; see Isa 59:2 and many other passages.

A new theme appears at vs. 9 (though there is a verbal link with 7; the initial word is *gādar* in both verses): God has "blocked up" and "made crooked" the sufferer's "path"—in non-figurative language, God has frustrated his purposes and kept him from pursuing the kind of life he wanted. Job 3:23 and Hosea 2:6[8H] also speak of God's blocking up a person's path, and Ps 146:9 speaks of God's twisting the way of the wicked (cf. vs. 11 below and for a verbal parallel Jer 3:21). Just why "cut stones" (*gāzīt*) should be mentioned specifically is uncertain, but the idea may be that this material, used only in the finest, most substantial buildings in ancient Israel, is specified in order to indicate that God has walled the man in as solidly as possible. Weiser paraphrases by saying that the man finds himself in a cul-de-sac no matter where he turns. The path motif may have provided the transition to the picture of God as a bear and lion, the idea being that these predators lie in wait beside a man's path.

The bear and lion, frequently mentioned together as the most dangerous of all beasts, are figurative for a man's enemies also, for example, in Pss 22:13[14H] and 10:9 (the latter passage is close to the present verse in that the lion is said to lie in wait for its prey). Occasionally God in his anger is compared to a bear or lion, cf. Isa 38:13 and especially Hosea 13:8, which is very similar to the present passage.

The vivid picture of God deliberately setting up a helpless man as his target recurs in Job 16:12–13; cf. Job 6:4; Ps 38:2[3H]; Lam 2:4. The main point of the picture is simply that God assails a man, but it is also possible that the poet meant to suggest that God afflicts man with sickness, since "arrows" are rather often figurative for disease; cf. e.g. Job 34:6; Ps 91:5, and the memorable scene at the beginning of the *Iliad,* in which the archer Apollo shoots shafts of pestilence into the Greek camp. These verses

(12–13) are linked to the foregoing not by sense but by sound: 11 begins *dᵉrākay* and 12 *dārak*.

The cruel laughter of the man's own people (see NOTE) is part of what he had to endure. This is mentioned again in vs. 63; for other parallels see COMMENT on 1:7. The specific reference to taunting *songs* recurs at vs. 63 and in Job 30:9. Reference to having to drink bitter things (vs. 15) was also apparently a commonplace image for suffering; cf. vs. 19 and Jer 9:15[14H]; Job 9:18.

Since both verbs used in vs. 16 are very rare, and of somewhat uncertain meaning, it is not clear exactly what picture is intended. It seems likely that approximately the same situation is depicted in both parts of the line. If so, there are many parallels in laments to "trampling in the dirt," for example, Ps 7:5[6H], and "he ground my teeth in the gravel" may be an equivalent for the more common "lick the dust," cf. Ps 72:9; Micah 7:17, and also 102:9[10H].

As stated above, then, the poet has to this point presented the plaint of a sufferer in pictures which are conventional and typical rather than sharply individual. We are thus prevented from identifying the speaker with any specific man, and compelled to believe that the writer intended something other than a portrait of a contemporary: he meant to show human suffering as it is commonly and generally felt by men in the dark times when God appears as an enemy. For a time he deliberately draws attention away from the particular events of 587 B.C., as if to say: Look—this is what any man may go through.

The following passage (vss. 17–21) is transitional. Now the man tells of his inner reaction to all his suffering: he is led to despair, and then to hope. The sentence with which he sums up the situation: "I thought, 'My lasting hope in Yahweh has perished,'" is already a hint that a turning point is coming, because this sort of direct speech, beginning, "I thought (said) . . ." is occasionally used in laments at just such points. Thus in Jonah 2:4[5H]: "So I said, 'I have been driven from your sight.' Yet I will continue to look to your holy temple." Very similar are Pss 31:23[22H]; 94:18; 139:11; cf. also Isa 6:5; 38:11; 49:4.

Depending on the translation adopted for vss. 19–20 (see NOTES), the expression of a hopeful attitude either follows at once, at vs. 19, or as translated here, begins at vs. 21, after an amplified

description of the man's inner despondency (vss. 19–20). The one
cause for hope is the mercy of Yahweh (his *ḥesed,* "steadfast love,"
or "loyal love"). This is not a passing phase in God, but an
enduring part of his nature, always being renewed toward mankind,
and an ancient part of Israel's faith. Quite appropriately Weiser
compares God's description of his nature (Exod 34:6–7), in the
course of his appearance to Moses on Sinai: "Yahweh, a god
merciful and gracious, patient, and abounding in mercy and faithfulness." On the basis of this enduring mercy the speaker asserts
that even in trials Yahweh is "his share." The expression arises
in the traditions about the division of the Promised Land. All the
Israelites received allotments, but not the priests, for God said to
Aaron (Num 18:20): "I am your portion." At the most literal
level this meant that the priests were to live from offerings, but
the expression came to be a way of asserting that when every
other support for life failed, Yahweh remained: "My flesh and
my heart may fail, but God is . . . my portion forever" (Ps 73:26).
Not God's love, but his anger is a passing phase, and thus even
of suffering the first word of faith can be "Good"; the poet puts
this "good" (Heb. *ṭōb*) at the beginning of the next three lines
(vss. 25–27). It is good to wait in hope for Yahweh's mercy
to show itself. It is good for a man if he has to carry the yoke of
trials (cf. 1:14). "In his youth" (or "from his youth," as the phrase
might also be rendered) seems to stress that suffering has educa-
tional value, just as, in the Israelite view, corporal punishment
was good for the young (Prov 13:24; 22:15; 23:13–14; 29:15).
The phrase "in his youth" is thus not to be pressed for biographical
information about the speaker; it is, as Albrektson notes, a general,
almost proverbial observation.

When suffering comes, a man should be passive and utterly
abase himself before God. To "put the mouth in the dirt," was
an age-old act of obeisance and of humiliation before a superior
among the peoples of the ancient Near East (cf. Micah 7:17; Ps
72:9). It is implied that this prostration is before Yahweh, hence
one ought probably to understand the expression "the one who
strikes him" in vs. 30 as a reference to Yahweh rather than to
a human. Though Luther in translating this passage deliberately
omitted the "Maybe" from "Maybe there is hope" as too faint-
hearted for properly robust faith, this phrase is not so much an
expression of wavering faith as a recognition that God is sovereign

and free; it is the voice of piety, not of doubt. Ancient Israelites rather often said "Maybe" about the possibility that Yahweh will act favorably in a given case (Exod 32:30; Num 23:3, 27; Josh 14:12, etc.) or for similar reasons they say "Who knows?" (II Sam 12:22; Joel 2:14; Jonah 3:9).

The degree of humility required of man is deliberately stated in extreme terms, so as to prepare for the forceful statement—a threefold "because"—of the reasons for patient trust. God does not cast off forever, and though he inflicts pain it is followed by compassion. Afflicting people is not deliberate on his part; literally translated, the text says (vs. 33) it is not "from his heart."

This is a kind of resolution in advance of the paradox that is stated in vss. 37–38: both good and bad happen by command of God. While this is true, as it must be since God is the creator who "spoke and it was done" (vs. 37; cf. Num 23:19), yet suffering, pain, and evil are not his final intention. He does not act like a tyrant, mistreating prisoners and denying men justice. The lines that assert this (34–36; see NOTE) seem to draw on traditional descriptions of unjust rule. The tyrant king of Babylon "did not let his prisoners go home" (Isa 14:17; text somewhat uncertain). Yahweh's concern for the imprisoned, in contrast, is frequently mentioned: for example, Pss 68:6[7H]; 69:33[34H]; 107:10–16. "The prisoners of the earth" is probably a reference to prisoners in general (cf. $^{a}n\bar{\imath}yy\bar{e}$ '$ere\d{s}$, Job 24:4) rather than to "the prisoners of the land (Judah)," which would be a reference to the captives in Babylon. There are many biblical references to perversion of justice by rulers and associated with this one occasionally finds it stated that the wicked imagine "Yahweh does not see" (Pss 64:5[6H]; 94:2–7; Ezek 9:9; cf. Isa 47:10; Ezek 8:12; Isa 29:15; Jer 12:4). This may account for the presence here of the clauses "before the Most High" and "without the Lord seeing," which are slightly incongruous in a sentence describing the Lord, but the whole verse is syntactically difficult (see NOTE) and the interpretation uncertain.

God is, after all, the creator (vs. 37), and though he brings about both good things and bad things (calamities, trouble, not moral evil, cf. Amos 3:6), this reference to his creative omnipotence is intended as comforting, because the creator and what he has made cannot in the final analysis be evil. Hence the speaker turns to consider man's proper response, in a line which looks both forward and back. By repeating the "man" of vs. 1, it rounds off the poem and calls attention to the progress in thought to this point. We have come from a complaint beginning "I am the man," through hopeful submission, to the conclusion "Why should a man complain?" (vs. 39). A new note is added with the reference to "his sins." Even though the sense here is: "what his sins have brought on him" (see BDB, s.v. *ḥēṭ'*, no. 3; cf. Ps 38:3[4H]; Zech 14:19), this is the first time it is implied in the poem that the man's troubles have been due to his own sins, that he should call into question not the goodness of God but his own goodness. Thus the line leads into the ensuing call for repentance.

The brief summons to repentance calls for three things: self-examination, repentance—the usual term "return" is employed—and sincerity. Sincerity is demanded in the phrase "let us lift our heart along with our hands," (vs. 41), which emphasizes that the inner attitude must accompany the outward gesture. The intent is much like the familiar "Rend your heart and not your garments" of Joel 2:13.

Rather unobtrusively the plural of the exhortation ("Let us") is carried over into the prayer that follows: "We have rebelled." The result, however, is a major shift in point of view. Suddenly the voice of the whole people is heard, and the concern is once again that of the previous chapters, the ruin of the nation. It seems best to regard all of vss. 42–66 as belonging to this collective prayer, in spite of the obviously disparate elements. The prayer is not entirely made up of explicit petitions for help, since there is a good deal describing distress, but this is a normal feature of collective laments, a good example being chapter 5 of this book. Note that in spite of superficial resemblance to lines in the complaint which began the present chapter, we are really at a different stage. There the idea was to depict a man's troubles so as to show his inner progress from despair to hope, whereas here suffering is described in order to awaken Yahweh's pity—all is turned toward God. The "we" which begins the prayer is maintained only as far as vs. 47. Thereafter the poet speaks, in the first-person singular, as one observing the ruin of his people (vss. 48–51). This point of view is abandoned in turn in favor of subjective description of the troubles and petition, but this time not in first plural ("we"), but in singular ("I"). This is a return to the style of the first part of the chapter, but the introduction of the whole people in the preceding section brings the collective sense much more strongly to the fore than was true in the earlier section, and hence one may think of this "I" passage as a continuation and completion of the collective prayer. It may appear inconsistent to make a distinction between the "I" of the end and the "I" of the beginning of the poem, but it seems justified when one recalls that someone reading the poem, or a worshiper hearing it in a service, experiences the poem serially, starting at the beginning, and is not likely to have the end in mind at the start.

The first line of the prayer (vs. 42) states the basic situation: we have rebelled, and you have not forgiven, as is evident from what has happened and still is happening to us. You have slain us unsparingly (cf. 2:21), and then shut out our prayers for help (vs. 44; for parallels see vs. 8 above). The reference to God's wrapping himself in "cloud" (*'ānān*) may be merely a picturesque metaphor, but more likely this is a reference to a permanent part of Yahweh's nature, as Israel conceived it: he is enveloped by a radiant *'ānān,* through which he reveals himself, by which he overwhelms enemies, and in which he may hide himself, as here. Similar conceptions of deities were held in Mesopotamia and Canaan. The subject has been dealt with extensively by Professor George Mendenhall in public lectures that are soon to be published. Reference to Israel's enemies at the end of the stanza (vs. 45) leads over into the next: "All our enemies sneer at us." (For this stock motif see COMMENT on 2:15.) The next line is a variant on stock expressions which must have been proverbial in ancient Israel, to judge from their recurrence in the Old Testament (Isa 24:17–18; Jer 48:43–44) and the alliteration and assonance of the Hebrew (*paḥad wāpaḥat . . . haššē't wᵉhaššeber;* the translation "panic and pit, wreck and ruin" attempts to suggest the effect). Such assonance is a characteristic of pairs of words in certain Hebrew idioms, much as in English "house and home."

The point of view changes and for a brief space the poet speaks of his grief at the ruin of his people (vss. 48–51). He will weep unceasingly (cf. 1:16; 2:18; Ps 119:136) until Yahweh looks down in pity. Though the connection to the rest of the prayer is loose, this indirect appeal does supply a link to the context.

The lament and prayer resumes at vs. 52, except that as stated, the prayer is cast in the singular. Briefly the theme of suffering is touched on. The themes are traditional: he is being hunted like a bird (cf. e.g. Pss 11:1; 124:7; 140:5[6H]; Jer 16:16; and cf. COMMENT on 1:13), and has been thrown into a pit and—a motif that seems to be unparalleled—they throw stones down at him. The infernal connotations of the word "pit" are taken up in the next line when it is said that waters came up over his head. These are the waters of Sheol, a traditional image for really desperate trouble; cf. Jonah 2:5–6[6–7H]; II Sam 22:5–6=Pss 18:4–5[5–6H]; 69:1–2, 14–15[2–3, 15–16H]. In the first part of the chapter, Yahweh himself was the enemy, but now there is reference to "Those who are my enemies for no reason." This echoes "our enemies" in vs. 46, and touches a theme which dominates the remainder of the chapter: Yahweh is to help against the enemies. If it is correct to understand the "I" in this part of the poem as collective, then the enemies are foreign: Babylon and Edom (cf. 4:21–22).

The reference to the pit and to the infernal waters sets the stage for the *De Profundis* which follows, in which even the language is strikingly similar to that of the familiar psalm (cf. vss. 55–56 and Ps 130:1–2; see NOTE). In every way at his command the speaker begs Yahweh to listen, observe, help, and take up his cause against his enemies, who constantly plot against him, deny him his rights, and mock him. All that is asked is that they be treated as they have treated their fellow man. This is the longest exposition of such an idea in Lamentations; shorter presentations of it occur at 1:21–22 and 4:21–22. That God should deal out retribution to Israel's enemies, or torment to a man's tormentors, is a typical Old Testament theme. Even when Israel was conscious of her own rebellion against God, as in this poem (vss. 39–42), and acknowledged the justice of such punishment as was meted out to her, this never meant to her that her enemies were justified in the atrocities they committed. On the contrary, belief in divine justice meant that Yahweh should deal just as strictly with the nations as he did with Israel.

IV
A SURVIVOR'S ACCOUNT
(4:1–22)

Aleph	1 How gold is despised! Good gold is hated! Jewels are scattered about at every street corner!
Beth	2 The people of Zion, once so precious, worth their weight in fine gold, Are now treated like cheap crockery, the work of the potter.
Gimel	3 Even a jackal will offer her teats and suckle her cubs, But my people is truly cruel, like the ostriches in the desert.
Daleth	4 The tongue of the sucking child, from thirst, sticks to its palate. Young children ask for bread; no one gives it to them.
He	5 Those who once fed on delicacies are destitute in the streets; Those brought up in scarlet clothing pick through garbage.
Waw	6 So the wickedness of my people was greater than the sin of Sodom, Which was overthrown in a moment, without a hand laid on it.
Zayin	7 Her Nazirites were whiter than snow, lighter than milk. Their bodies were more ruddy than corals; their beards were lapis lazuli.

Heth 8 Now they look blacker than soot; they are not
recognized in the street.
Their skin has shrunk over their bones, has
become dry as wood.

Teth 9 Those killed by the sword had it better than
those killed by famine,
Those who perished of wounds, than those
who lacked the fruits of the field.

Yod 10 With their own hands the kindly women
cooked their children.
That was the food they had, when my
people was ruined.

Kaph 11 Yahweh gave full vent to his rage, he poured
out his hot anger,
And he set fire to Zion that burned its
foundations.

Lamed 12 The kings of the earth could not believe, nor
could any of the world's rulers,
That enemies and foes would pass
through the gates of Jerusalem.

Mem 13 On account of the sins of her prophets, the
iniquities of her priests,
Who shed within her the blood of
innocent men,

Nun 14 They wandered blind in the streets, defiled
with blood;
By exertion they are spent and
exhausted; their clothing is tattered.

Samekh 15 "Get away! Unclean!" they call to them.
"Get away! Don't touch!"
"For they have gone away and must
wander," they say. "They shall no longer
abide among the nations."

Pe 16 The splendor of Yahweh destroyed them. He
stopped looking after them.
He did not respect the priests, or spare the
elders.

Ayin   17 We kept awake and wore out our eyes looking
                for help—in vain.
            On our lookout we kept watch for a
                nation that does not save.

Sade   18 They hunted our steps so we could not walk
                in our streets.
            Our end drew near, our time was up, and
                our end came.

Qof   19 Our pursuers were swifter than eagles in the sky.
            They were hot after us in the mountains;
                they lay in ambush for us in the desert.

Resh   20 The breath of our nostrils, the anointed of
                Yahweh, was caught in their traps,
            The one of whom we said, "In his shadow
                we will live among the nations."

Sin   21 Rejoice and be glad, O Edom, you who dwell
                in Uz,
            The cup will come round to you also, and
                you will get drunk and strip naked.

Taw   22 Your punishment is complete, O Zion! He will
                not exile you again.
            May he punish your iniquity, O Edom!
            May he lay bare your sins!

4:1. *is despised . . . is hated!* Translation is based on emending MT *yū'ām* to *yū'āb,* and repointing of *yišne'* to *yiśśānē'* (so already Ehrlich, *Randglossen;* Ehrlich, however, emends the first verb to *yizzā'ēm,* "is cursed"). Ordinarily the text has been rendered: "How the gold has grown dim; how the pure gold has changed!" following the ancient versions, but though linguistically possible this does not yield satisfactory sense: (a) Gold does not tarnish or grow dark in any striking way, one of its principal qualities being that it stays bright. Figurative language involving gold in the Old Testament never otherwise makes reference to the color or brightness of gold; the point of the comparison is always the *value* of gold. (b) The first line of vs. 1 must fit with the second, and with vs. 2 as well, for the "gold" image is resumed there, and explained as applying to the men of Zion. But with the stones of 1b and the men of vs. 2, the idea is that something happens to them from without, not that there is an internal change. As usually translated, the image in 1a is out of harmony with what follows. In favor of the conjecture proposed here, note: (a) change of *yišne'* to *yiśśānē'* does not involve any change of consonants; in fact, it accounts for the otherwise anomalous *aleph* of the MT. The Niphal of *śānē'* occurs at Prov 14:20 (possibly also 14:17); (b) *śānē',* "to hate," occurs as a parallel to, or in association with, *tō'ēbāh,* "abomination," or *tā'ēb,* "to abominate," in Prov 6:16; Ps 119:163; Amos 5:10; Deut 12:31; (c) interchange of *mem* and *beth* is attested as a scribal error fairly commonly; in this case error in the rarer word would have preceded and necessitated the reinterpretation of *yiśśānē'* to *yišne'.* On the derivation of *hō'īb* see NOTE at 2:1; (d) The translation yields a consistent image, the point throughout being that what is intrinsically precious is treated as worthless.

Jewels. *'abnē qōdeš,* if understood as "holy stones," is a puzzling phrase, especially since commentators are right in rejecting the idea that this could be a reference to the stones of the temple. Without emending the text, J. A. Emerton explains *qōdeš* not as "holy" but as "jewel, ornament," on the basis of Aramaic, Arabic, and Akkadian cognates, and his suggestion has been adopted here; see "The Meaning of *'abnē qōdeš* in Lamentations 4:1," ZAW 79 (1967), 233–36. On the possible Akkadian cognate see now also K. Deller, "Die Briefe des Adad-šumu-uṣur," in *lišān mitḫurti,* ed. W. Röllig, Alter Orient und Altes Testament, I (Kevelaer and Neukirchen-Vluyn, 1968), p. 53. Julius Wellhausen, *Skizzen und Vorarbeiten,* V, 2d ed. (Berlin, 1893), 184, arrived at the sense "jewels" by taking "holy stones" as meaning "amulets." For comparison of a person to a jewel, cf. "The Babylonian Theodicy," lines 56–57: "O palm, tree of wealth, my precious brother / Endowed with all wisdom, jewel of gold." Cf. also Song of Songs 5:11–15, and the imagery in the Sumerian "Message of Ludingira to his Mother," extant in various copies, see Jean Nougayrol, *Ugaritica,* V (Paris, 1969), 310 ff. ("Signalement lyrique") and literature cited there; also W. Heimpel, *Die Tierbilder in der sumerischen Literatur,* Studia Pohl 2 (Rome, 1968), pp. 60–63. (I am indebted to my colleague, J. S. Cooper, for these references.)

at every street corner. Hebrew literally "at the head of all the streets"; cf. Isa 51:20; Lam 2:19d.

2. *worth their weight.* For this translation of the difficult *mesullā'īm* cf. Job 28:16, 19.

3. *jackal.* Hebrew "the jackals." The plural ending *-īn* instead of the usual *-īm* occurs here as also in 1:4. There is no need to see here the word *tannīn(īm),* "sea-monster" or "whale," as is done in the New English Bible, apparently based on G. R. Driver, "Mythical Monsters in the Old Testament," *Studi orientalistici in onore di G. Levi della Vida,* I (Rome, 1956), 246. Gr. *drakontes* rests on a confusion.

offer. Heb. *ḥāleṣū,* "draw out," probably transferred from human behavior rather than characteristic of the animal.

my people. "Daughter of my people"; see Introduction. Some emend to "daughters (plural) of my people," *benōt,* on the ground that this applies only to the women, but that seems over-literal. Note however that it is unusual to find *bat 'ammī* first in a line.

truly cruel. Based on taking *l* in *le'akzār* as emphatic *lamed,* as first proposed by Israel Eitan, "Hebrew and Semitic Particles— Continued," *American Journal of Semitic Languages and Literatures* 45 (1928), 202. Cf. McDaniel, *Biblica* 49 (1968), 206–8. 4Q179 II 4 reads *bt 'my 'kzryh.*

ostriches. Reading *kaye'ēnīm* with Qre, etc.

5. *pick through garbage.* Literally "have embraced refuse-heaps."

6. The verse begins with *waw*-consecutive; see NOTE on 1:6.

my people. "Daughter of my people"; see Introduction.

without a hand laid on it. MT *we'lō' ḥālū bāh yādāyim* is very difficult. The translation here follows the main lines of the explanation proposed by McDaniel, *Biblica* 49 (1968), 45–48, who cites passages in the "War of the Sons of Light with the Sons of Darkness" (Qumran *Milḥama* [War Scroll], 1QM) which seem to establish a sense "attack" for this combination of words (1QM, col. 1:1; 9:1; 16:5–6; 16:7, *yḥlw ydm lhpyl bḥlly ktyym;* 17:12–14). It is perhaps best to leave open the question as to the root of *ḥālū,* and the exact form to be read in this passage, whether MT or something else, since the new evidence does not seem to settle these questions. The present writer differs from McDaniel also in preferring to understand *lō'* simply as the negative. The sense (see COMMENT) is that Sodom was destroyed without the extra suffering involved in a protracted siege. Other commentators have favored the same general sense, but reach it by different routes. For contrasting proposals, see Rudolph, Fitzgerald, CBQ 29 (1967), 368–69, and Robert Gordis, "Commentary on the Text of Lamentations (Part Two)," JQR 58 (1967–68), 14–33.

7. *Her Nazirites.* Commentators have often changed "Nazirites" to "youths," *ne'āreḥā;* the change is slight, involving only one letter, but the objections to "Nazirites" are not compelling. This could be a straightforward reference to Nazirites, that is, men under a special vow to abstain from wine and from contact with the dead, and to let their hair grow long; if not, the term may be used here in the sense "champion, chief," as in the ancient poems Gen 49:26 and Deut 33:16, where Joseph is called the *nāzīr* of his brethren. In that case the present verse would refer to young nobles.

Their bodies. The usual translation for *'eṣem* in this passage, "bodies," is adopted here as fitting the context well, but the Hebrew word normally means bone(s), and the translation glosses over a genuine problem. Passages in which *'eṣem* may stand for the whole person (e.g. Prov 15:30; 16:24) are not completely satisfactory parallels, since they never involve a comparison as the present text does, and since here the quality compared—redness—is rather incongruous with "bones" as the subject.

their beards. Heb. *gizrātām* has long been recognized as a problem. The present translation of this rare word is not based on an etymological explanation, but on what is said in similar contexts. The word must refer to a part of the body which can be compared to lapis lazuli, a dark blue stone. Ancient sculptors and ivory carvers often represented hair on carved heads by inlaid lapis lazuli, and ancient literature also adopts this practice in describing the appearance of gods and men. Thus Shamash has the epithet "Bearing a beard of . . . lapis lazuli"; see Åke W. Sjöberg and E. Bergmann, *The Collection of the Sumerian Temple Hymns,* Texts from Cuneiform Sources, III (Locust Valley, New York, 1969), line 173; on p. 87 Sjöberg gives parallels in Sumerian and Akkadian sources. Compare also Greek (Homer, etc.) *kyanochaitēs,* "dark-haired," and *kyanophrys,* "dark-browed," from *kyanos,* "dark-blue enamel, lapis lazuli." Note also the description of Re in the Egyptian text "Deliverance of Mankind from Destruction" (ANET, p. 11): "His bones were of silver, his flesh of gold, and his hair of genuine lapis lazuli." If not the beard or hair then *gizrātām* might refer to the eyebrows. In a Ugaritic epic, it is said of a beautiful woman: *dʿqh.ib.iqni.ʿp[ʿp]h/sp.ṯrml,* i.e. "Her eyebrows are pure lapis lazuli; her eyes are bowls of jet" (Krt 147–48). The translation "eyebrows" for *ʿqh* is based on the parallelism and artists' practice referred to above; an Egyptian text also refers to eyebrows of lapis lazuli, see C. H. Gordon, UT, Glossary ※1906. It is conceivable that *gizrātām* is an error for *gabbōtām,* "their brows"; *gabbōt ʿēnayim* occurs once, Lev 14:9, as the word for eyebrows. Löhr proposed *nizrātam;* Weiser, etymologizing *gizrātām* translates "tattoos." Note that Paffrath translated "hair" in the present passage.

9. *Those who perished . . . field.* The Hebrew is very difficult, and the translation is conjectural at numerous points. It seems relatively certain that *meduqqārīm,* "of wounds," literally "pierced, wounded," is parallel to *ḥallē,* "slain," of 9a, on the basis of Jer 51:4; the rest is very uncertain.

10. *the food.* Heb. *bārōt,* a *hapax legomenon,* is evidently a noun derived from *bārāh,* "to eat." Since Gordis has recently (JQR 58 [1967–68]) defended the old suggestion that MT *lᵉbārōt* conceals the designation of a Mesopotamian demon **labartu* (so also BH³, notes), it may be in place to repeat what was seen long ago, namely, that the Akkadian name in question must be read *la-maš-tu,* not *la-bar-tu.*

12. *rulers.* Literally "enthroned ones," Heb. *yōšᵉbē.* As in Amos 1:5, 8, the parallel word "kings" suggests the translation "rulers" rather than "dwellers." See Frank M. Cross, Jr., and David Noel Freedman, "The Song of Miriam," JNES 14 (1955), 248–49.

13. Since the preceding verse is complete, and cannot be joined to vs. 13, vs. 13, a prepositional phrase which cannot stand by itself, must be joined to vs. 14 which follows. Otherwise one must supply a subject and predicate "This happened" or the like (so Rudolph), but that seems inadmissible except as a last resort.

14. Verses 14 and 15 (together with vs. 13, which must begin the section; see preceding NOTE) are among the most difficult verses in the book, and no interpretation so far proposed (including that favored here) can claim to clear up all the problems in a completely convincing way. No review of the wide variety of proposals made by other commentators is given here, for which the reader may see Albrektson and Rudolph; some previous suggestions will be dealt with in connection with individual points. Read (vs. 14):

$$nā'ū\ \,'iwrīm\ baḥūṣōt\ nig'ᵃlū\ baddām$$
$$bil'ī\ kālū\ wayyīgᵉ'ū\ bā{<}lū{>}\ lᵉbušēhem$$

(a) If one connects 13 and 14, then *nā'ū* is hardly said of the priests and prophets, which would be odd syntax, and must then refer to the people of Zion. (b) *'iwrīm,* "blind men," is a bit odd, but in a somewhat similar description of a catastrophe we have "they walk like blind men" (Zeph 1:17; cf. Isa 59:10; Deut 28:29). (Syriac has "her nobles," best explained as from *śārīm* [*śrym*] for MT *'wrym* [see Albrektson]; this would yield good sense.) (c) Probably one should either read Niphal perfect *nig'ᵃlū,* as here, or else *gō'ᵃlū,* Pual perfect, instead of the odd composite form of MT, but cf. Isa 59:3. (d) In the second line, MT *bᵉlō yūkᵉlū yiggᵉ'ū bilbušēhem* is really not possible, though it has been defended. Rudolph: "What they were not allowed to, they touched with their garments"; others give "so that no one could touch their garments" (see Albrektson for details). (e) Redividing the consonantal text, *bil'ī* is taken to mean "by vain effort" positing the existence of a noun *lᵉ'ī* (like *ṣᵉbī*, *šᵉbī*, etc.) from *lā'āh*, "to be weary, toil"; cf. Aram. *lē'ū;* Syr. *le'ūtā*, "fatigue." Both *kālāh* and *yāga'* are regularly followed by *b* marking the cause of the exhaustion. (f) Deleting a *w, kālū* is from *kālāh*, "to be exhausted, at an end," and is followed by a form of *yāga'*, "to be weary." (g) Restoring *bā<lū>* (lost by haplography before another *l*): "their clothes are worn out." If the above conjectures are approximately correct, the picture is of people during or just after the siege: in shock, bloodstained, exhausted, and ragged. In their filth and raggedness they resemble lepers (who were required to tear their clothes, Lev 13:45–46), hence they are depicted as giving the lepers' cry or as greeted by the cry "Unclean!" (see NOTE on vs. 15 below).

15. This difficult verse is translated as if spoken by the enemies of the Israelites, the first line being addressed directly to them, the second spoken about them. Note, however, the following problems. (a) Both lines are exceptionally long, and quite possibly the text is not in order. (b) The meaning of *nāṣū* is very uncertain; the context seems to require an approximate synonym of *nā'ū*, literally "they have wandered." (c) Many translations join *baggōyīm*, "among the nations," to "they say"; the present translation takes *baggoyīm* with *lāgūr*, comparing vs. 20 and 1:3.

16. *The splendor of Yahweh.* Literally "the face of Yahweh." For God's face as hostile and threatening, compare Ps 34:16[17H]: "The face of the Lord is against (*'al*) the wicked," and Lev 20:3, 6; 26:17; Ezek 14:8; Ps 80:16[17H]. In a famous episode God shows Moses some of his glory, but not his face: "for no man can see me and live." See Mitchell Dahood, review of Albrektson's *Studies* in *Biblica* 44 (1963), 548; *Psalms I, 1–50*, first NOTE on Ps 34: 17; *Psalms II, 51–100*, third NOTE on Ps 80:17; "Hebrew-Ugaritic Lexicography, VIII," *Biblica* 51 (1970), 399–400. "Face," *pᵉnē*, grammatically a plural in Hebrew, is usually construed with a plural verb. Here it takes a singular verb; see GKC, para. 146a, for other cases where a verb agrees with the *rectum* of the construct chain, not the *regens*.

destroyed. On Heb. *hillēq*="to destroy" see KB³, s.v. *hlq* III, where Akk. *halāqu*, Ugar. *hlq*, Eth. *halqa* are compared. See also McDaniel, *Biblica* 49 (1968), 48, with references to observations by Patton and Dahood.

He did not respect, . . . spare. Where the translation has singulars, implying that Yahweh is the subject, MT has plurals: "They did not respect, . . . spare." Plurals make of this a reference to what the conquerors did. This fits the general context of the book, but the shift from line 1 of this same verse, where Yahweh is the destroyer, is abrupt, and it seems better to read singular verbs here. At some stage prior to the fixing of the MT, there was a tendency to alter passages which ascribed to God responsibility for evil and calamity. This was not done systematically, and the changes that can be detected are slight. The process is well exemplified in the MT of Psalms as compared to the Psalms Scroll from Qumran (11QPs^a): 119:71 MT "I was afflicted," cf. 11QPs^a "You (God) afflicted me"; 119:83 MT "I was like a bottle in the smoke," cf. 11QPs^a "You (God) made me" etc. For other examples in Lamentations see above, NOTE on 1:12. Compare also the *Tiqqune Sopherim.*

17. *We kept awake.* Neither Ktib *'wdynh* (*'ōdenāh*) (so also a fragmentary text of Lamentations from Qumran, 5QThr^b) nor Qre *'ōdēnū* really yields acceptable sense, though each has been defended. Rudolph views either as acceptable. Ktib he understands as "they (feminine) still are" (the reference being to "our eyes"); Qre he explains as "we still are" ("we" going with the first plural suffix of "our eyes"). He would translate either "We still wore out our eyes looking," or "Our eyes still grew exhausted." But this use of *'ōd*+suffix in a kind of absolute construction is actually unparalleled, and the explanation *ad hoc.* The present translation is based on assuming a confusion of *r* and *d;* read *'arnū,* "we watched, stayed awake," Qal perfect of *'ūr,* and supply a conjunction *w* before *tiklenāh.* The assumption is that after the error of writing *d* for *r* had occurred, vowel-letters then came to be written at the wrong places.

On our lookout. Or "From"; see Dahood, *Biblica* 51 (1970), 403.

18. *They hunted . . . streets.* The translation is literal; if MT is correct, this line might refer to a time after the city wall had been breached, when bands of Chaldaean soldiers cut down anyone who set foot in the streets. Otherwise, as Rudolph suggests, following Ginsburg and Ehrlich, read *ṣārū* from *ṣrr,* "to be narrow, cramped in"; the verb occurs with the subject *ṣaʿad,* "step," also in Prov 4:12; Job 18:7; the change from *d* to *r* and vice versa is one frequently made, and translate: "Our steps were so confined we could not go out in the open." See Rudolph for a fuller discussion,

and other opinions. Dahood's "our feet have ranged far (cf. Ugar. *ṣd*) without coming into our squares" (*Biblica* 44 [1963], 548) seems to force the Hebrew unidiomatically.

19. *were hot after us*. On this sense of *dālaq* cf. Ps 10:2.

20. *traps*. The Hebrew word is rare (only here and Ps 107:19 [20H], where there is a textual problem) and the form slightly suspect, but the meaning is not seriously in question, since the verb *lākad*, "to catch," is frequently used with words meaning trap, snare, net, and the like. Cf. especially Ezek 19:8.

21. *O Edom*. "Daughter Edom"; see Introduction.

22. *O Zion . . . O Edom!* "Daughter" is prefixed to each name; see Introduction.

COMMENT

This poem is also an alphabetic acrostic, with the acrostic figuring only in the first line of each stanza, as in chapters 1 and 3. The stanzas are, however, only two lines long, in contrast to the three-line stanzas in the preceding poems.

The content of the chapter contrasts markedly with that of earlier chapters, especially chapter 3, and one may plausibly suppose that this effect was intentional on the part of the author or editor of the book. The point of view is the same throughout, the speaker being someone who has been through the siege and fall of the city. His primary concern is to report the horrors that took place; briefer attention is given to the cause of the catastrophe and at the very end (vss. 21–22) there is an imprecation against Edom and a benediction on Zion. Although what the speaker relates is moving in its own way, the poem exhibits a relaxation of the more intense emotion of the earlier poems, and the vividness imparted there by the dramatic appearance of various speakers and especially by the personification of Zion is absent here. The tone is more matter-of-fact, closer to the actual events. In this respect it is like chapter 5, and no doubt the placing of these poems together at the end of the book was both deliberate and the product of careful reflection.

The poem consists of a series of observations, mostly having to do with the suffering of various classes of the population. There is little progression in thought, though vss. 18–20 do supply a climax of action, since they seem to refer to the final flight from the city and the capture of the king. The poem is then rounded off by a threat against Edom and a word of consolation for Israel. It is scarcely possible to outline the chapter beyond a sketch.

Outline

A. A survivor's account of the siege and fall of the city, vss. 1–20.
  1. The fate of different groups of people, 1–17.
  2. The fall of the city, the flight, the capture of the king, 18–20.
B. A concluding curse on Edom, and blessing on Zion, vss. 21–22.

The first two verses serve as a general introduction to the main theme of the chapter, the mistreatment of the people of Jerusalem. After the familiar *'ēkāh* ("How!") at the beginning, the writer creates a bit of suspense by starting off, not with a literal statement, but with highly figurative language which is explained only in the following stanza. Gold, which as the most precious of metals was a traditional literary figure for what is of highest value, is despised! Precious stones are being thrown in the gutter. That is, he explains (vs. 2), the people of Zion, worth more even than gold, have been treated like worthless broken dishes. The clay vessel, most common of ancient artifacts, as any excavation shows, was proverbial for cheapness. When one was broken the sherds were thrown out, not pieced together, and there was little regret over the loss; cf. Hosea 8:8; Jer 22:28; 48:38. Cf. 1:11: "How worthless I have become!"

The next eight stanzas take up the theme of famine, especially as it affected the most defenseless and dependent of the populace: the little children. As in Isa 1:3 and Jer 8:7, the people are compared unfavorably to animals. Even jackals (see NOTE), carrion eaters who haunt deserted ruins, nurse their cubs, but the people of Israel do not feed their children and are cruel as the ostrich. Here, of course, this indictment is ironic, for it is not the people's fault that they are unable to feed their children. If the ostrich is indeed referred to in a difficult passage in Job (39:13–18), we may conclude that it was ancient opinion that the female laid her eggs in the ground and unconcernedly left them to be trampled, so that the bird was proverbial for cruel treatment of its young.

For other ancient descriptions of famine and its effect, see 1:11, 19; 2:11–12, and parallels cited in the COMMENT there. Failing of milk in nursing mothers (and animals) in time of siege is specifically mentioned among the curses in a Sefîre treaty (eighth century B.C.): "[And should seven nurses] anoint [*their breasts* and] nurse a young boy, may he not have his fill; and should seven mares suckle a colt, may it not be sa[ted; and should seven] cows give suck to a calf, may it not have its fill; and should seven ewes suckle a lamb, [may it not be sa]ted," Sefîre I A 21–24, translation of J. A. Fitzmyer, *The Aramaic Inscriptions of Sefîre,* Biblica et Orientalia, 19 (Rome, 1967), p. 15. Compare especially the curse uttered by the god Era (*Era Epic* IV 121): "I will make the breast dry up, so that the baby shall not live." Note also Hosea 9:14 and cf. Hillers, *Treaty-Curses,* pp. 61–62.

The famine theme is continued by use of the "then and now" pattern, common in Lamentations (beginning at 1:1) and a staple element in funeral songs. Those who once could afford the best now hunt for scraps. "Scarlet clothing" was traditionally associated with being well-off. All the family of the "worthy woman" of Prov 31:21 wore scarlet. It is similarly linked with "delicacies" (*ma'adannîm*) in II Sam 1:24 (though there is a textual problem): Saul supplied the women of Jerusalem with scarlet clothing and "delicacies." A Mesopotamian proverb also associates a scarlet cloak (*ú-lap da-me*) with wealth, Lambert, *Babylonian Wisdom Literature,* p. 232, and in an Akkadian ritual which speaks of a god "who has given his city away" we read "The person who had good clothing perished of cold / He who owned vast fields perished of hunger," in "Ritual to be Followed by the *Kalû*-Priest when Covering the Temple Kettle-Drum," translated by A. Sachs, ANET, p. 337; Text D ii 1–5. Compare the "Curse of Agade," ANET, p. 651, lines 248–49: "May the princely children who ate (only) the very best bread, lie about in the grass, / May your man who used to carry off the first *fruits,* eat the *scraps* of his tables, the leather thongs of the door of his father's house" (translation of S. N. Kramer).

Since Jerusalem suffered so from famine during the protracted siege, the writer is compelled to conclude that her wickedness was greater than that of Sodom. Sodom also perished, but in an instant, not in long-drawn-out agony (see third NOTE on vs. 6). Compare vs. 9: "Those killed by the sword had it better than those killed by famine." Both the sinfulness of Sodom (Deut 32:32; Isa 1:10; 3:9; Jer 23:14; Ezek 16:46–56) and its sudden destruction (Deut 29:23[22H]; Isa 1:9; 13:19; Jer 49:18; 50:40; Amos 4:11; Zeph 2:9) were proverbial.

From the fate of the children, the poet turns to a group of especially sacred persons, the Nazirites (if the text and translation are correct, see NOTES on vs. 7). Again the "then and now" pattern is

used to show the ravages of famine. Once their skin was clear and
fair; their bodies ruddy like corals, and their beards (or eyebrows
or hair, see NOTE) like lapis lazuli. While details of the line are
uncertain (see NOTE), the general sense is clear. Also in Song of
Songs 5:10 the beloved is called "fair and ruddy" (*ṣaḥ weʾādōm*)
and the lover who is speaking passes from description of his com-
plexion (vs. 10) to his hair. In the same passage, parts of the body
are compared to precious stones, as here (cf. NOTE). On "ruddy,"
cf. the description of the youth David (*ʾadmōnī;* I Sam 16:12;
17:42). The change in their appearance is drastic. (For the effect
of starvation on the skin, cf. vs. 8 and Job 30:30). Sudden death—
even violent death—would have been better (vs. 9) than such slow
wasting away from hunger (see NOTE) which led to inhuman atrocities: women ate their own children. Though this may in fact have
happened in the siege of Jerusalem in 587/86, the writer may also
have been influenced by age-old literary tradition, in which the
stock description of famine included cannibalism as the last dreadful
state; see COMMENT on 1:11. Since this is one of the curses for
disobedience to the covenant, according to Deut 28:53–57 (which
resembles the present passage in formulation), it may be that the
writer intended to imply that Jerusalem was seeing the curse fulfilled
because of her disobedience; cf. COMMENT on 1:5.

As if a climax of horror had been reached, the writer turns to a
more general and less vivid summary statement. Yahweh has given
full vent to his anger, which in an exceptionally common metaphor
is called "fire." Cf. Deut 32:22; Isa 10:17; Jer 17:27; 21:14; 49:27;
50:32; Hosea 8:14; Amos 1:4, 7, 10, 12, 14; Lam 2:3, 5. The
line could be a reference to the actual fire which burned down the
city at the conquest, but over and above that, "fire" is symbolic of
the destructive wrath of God. This is especially apparent from the
reference to burning of the city's "foundations." Since stone foundations do not burn, this is not a literal statement; it calls to mind the
very similar description of Yahweh's fiery cosmic rage which "de-
vours the world and what it brings forth, and burns up the foundations of the mountains" (Deut 32:22).

Since the fall of Jerusalem in 587 B.C. can scarcely have been uni-
versally noticed by the kings and rulers of the earth, vs. 12 is not a
literal statement, but a way of stating the drastic, unexpected reversal
that has taken place. The theory widely held within Israel was that
Jerusalem was impregnable, immune to conquest, not so much be-

cause of its actual defenses as because it was "the holy dwelling place of the Most High" (Ps 46:4[5H]). In semi-mythical language the psalms describe how Zion and her king by the help of God beat back the assaults of all the kings of the earth. "God is known in her towers as a sure defense. For lo! the kings assembled, they came together. They beheld and were amazed; they were upset and put to flight. Trembling took hold of them, pangs like labor pains" (Ps 48:3–6[4–7H]). In this kind of religious thought, Zion is of world-wide, even cosmic significance, and thus at its fall, kings who stood in awe of her are thunderstruck.

The blame for Jerusalem's fall is assigned to her religious leaders, her prophets and priests, as also in 2:14. Here, by a bold simplifica-tion, they are said to have shed innocent blood within the city. This is elsewhere commonly pointed at as the sin of the rulers and judges (e.g. II Kings 21:16; Jer 22:17; Ezek 22:6, 27) or of the whole people (e.g. Jer 7:6; Ezek 33:25; Ps 106:38–39), but here, though the writer's idea is probably not that the priests and prophets them-selves laid violent hands on the righteous, he does assert that they were ultimately responsible for it by their whitewashing of injustice (cf. 2:14). The two verses that follow seem to be connected with this indictment of the religious leaders, but the Hebrew text is exceptionally uncertain (see NOTE) so that no interpretation yet proposed is free from difficulties. As interpreted by many, the un-named subject of vss. 14–15 is the priests and prophets mentioned in vs. 13: once "holier than thou" they are defiled by blood and are shunned like lepers. As translated here, the people as a whole are spoken of. "On account of the sins of her (Israel's) prophets . . . they (the Israelites) are defiled with blood," etc. This seems to fit best with 15b, which must refer to the nation as a whole, but certainty is scarcely attainable in view of the textual difficulties. In any case, the theme of defilement by blood runs through the three stanzas, a motif well-attested elsewhere. In priestly theology, blood defiles and pollutes the land, "and no atonement can be made on behalf of the land for the blood that has been shed in it, except by the blood of him who shed it" (Num 35:33). Similarly Ps 106:38–39, and especially Ezekiel (22:1–5) refer to the shedding of innocent blood as having defiled the land and its people. In the passage under dis-cussion, blood shed in the past (vs. 13) is avenged by the blood which now stains the people. Men wander uncertainly in the streets, like blind men (cf. Zeph 1:17), spattered with blood; presumably the writer has in mind scenes just before the final fall of the city, or just after the Chaldaeans entered it. They are worn and spent, and also their clothes are worn out. Their whole appearance suggests that of lepers, and the poet pictures them as greeted by the cry "Unclean!" People conclude that they have been shattered as a people and made exiles for good. Like lepers they must live apart, outside the "camp" as it were (Lev 13:46).

Yahweh has turned his "face," his overpowering splendor, toward his people in anger, not grace, and destroyed them (vs. 16). He had no respect for those one might have thought inviolable because of their sacred office or their age, the priests and elders.

Up to this point, a personal note has been struck only very lightly with almost casual first-person pronouns in the stock phrase "(daughter of) my people" (vss. 3, 6, 10). Now the personal, eyewitness element comes much more strongly to the fore in a series of verses which use "we" and identify the speaker very closely with his people. In vain, he says, speaking of the days just before the city fell, they had worn out their eyes looking for help from Egypt (Jer 37:5–10), who once again proved herself a "broken reed" (Isa 36:6). As we know from Jeremiah (34:21–22; 37:5–11), the Babylonian army was at one point drawn away from Jerusalem temporarily by the advance of an Egyptian army; as Jeremiah predicted, the relief to the city was ephemeral. The Egyptians did not save them, and the Babylonians returned as the prophet Jeremiah had predicted. This and the following verse (through vs. 20) are often cited as evidence against Jeremiah's authorship of Jeremiah, and indeed it is difficult to imagine him—even for poetic purposes—assuming the pose of someone who entertained high hopes of help from Egypt, or of one who set great store by King Zedekiah.

As the siege wore on, the confinement became more and more oppressive (vs. 18), and it was clear that the end was near. It came when the wall was breached, ending any hope of defense. "On the ninth of the month, the famine in the city had become so severe there was no food for the people of the land, and a breach had been made in the city. So all the soldiers fled, going out of the city by night by a gate between the double wall beside the royal garden, the Chaldaeans being all around the city. They went toward the Arabah. But the Chaldaeans pursued the king and caught up with him in the plain of Jericho, and all his army was scattered away from him, and they captured the king" (Jer 52:6–9; II Kings 25:3–6; cf. Jer 39:

1–5). The next verses of our poem seem to refer to this last desperate flight. It has been suggested that the author of Lamentations took part in the flight; while this remains conjectural, the vividness of the description would certainly permit such a supposition. It seems that the writer stood fairly close to King Zedekiah, and was much grieved at his capture (vs. 20). To be sure, he deliberately uses somewhat exaggerated language in speaking of the king, in order to sharpen the contrast between their hopes in the king and the bitter actuality. The king is called "the breath of our nostrils," an expression current in Canaan almost a thousand years earlier, as we know from the Amarna letters. This expression presumably was kept alive in the royal court in Jerusalem, though this is the only biblical use of the term. The "shadow" of the king is another of these court titles ascribing nearly divine status to the king (Pss 17:8; 91:1), just as "anointed of Yahweh" emphasizes the special standing of the king before God. Both terms, "breath" and "shadow," are ultimately related to Egyptian language concerning Pharaoh, the divine king; Ramses II, for example, is called "the breath of our nostrils" in an inscription at Abydos, and in another inscription he is titled "the beautiful falcon who protects his subjects with his wings and spreads shade over them"; see Jean de Savignac, "Theologie pharaonique et messianisme d'Israël," VT 7 (1957), 82; cf. Hermann Grapow, *Die bildlichen Ausdrücke des Aegyptischen* (Leipzig, 1924), pp. 45–46. Compare also Mesopotamian references to the shadow of the king, studied by A. Leo Oppenheim, "Assyriological Gleanings IV," *Bulletin of the American Schools of Oriental Research* 107 (Oct. 1947), 7–11. There is a poetic purpose in the use of these lofty titles, yet there is no reason to believe they are employed ironically or insincerely, especially since this is given prominent place as the climax of the tragic fall of the nation. It is hard to believe that Jeremiah could have written this.

The book of Obadiah in particular provides the background for the curse on Edom which follows. "When strangers seized (Jacob's) wealth, and foreigners entered his gates, and cast lots for Jerusalem, you were like one of them" (Obad 11; cf. also Ps 137:7; Ezek 35; Joel 3[4H]:19–21). From a "brother"—the descendants of Esau according to ancient tradition—this was intolerable treachery, and as in previous chapters (3:60–66; 1:21–22) the poet, though conscious of his own nation's sin, prays that divine justice will overtake the enemies of his people also. He does so here in an ironic command

to Edom to enjoy herself now, since soon she will have to drink
the cup of Yahweh's anger. This striking image for the divine anger
is found also in Jer 13:13; 25:15–29; 48:26; 49:12; 51:7, 39; Obad
16; Pss 60:3[5H]; 75:8[9H]; Hab 2:15–16; Zech 12:2; Job
21:20. The origin and precise meaning of this imagery is uncertain,
though in the present writer's opinion one may reject the suggestion
made by some that there is a connection to the jealousy ritual of
Num 5. There seems to be a parallel in the Sumerian "Curse of
Agade," line 228–29, as translated by S. N. Kramer, ANET, p.
650: (May certain cult-figures) "Lie prostrate like huge (fighting)
men drunk with wine." It may be that the image is a traditional
literary metaphor, rather than having anything to do with ritual.
On the subject see also John Bright, *Jeremiah,* AB, vol. 21 (New
York, 1965), NOTE on Jer 35:15. The association of drunkenness and self-exposure occurs also in Gen 9:21–22; Hab 2:15–16.
The threat to Edom is interrupted by a blessing on Zion. Apparently
the verb *tam,* "is over," is to be taken as referring to past time, the
sense being "The worst of your punishment is over, O Zion," though
in this context one might also take the perfect as precative. Though
this line, even if read as a declarative sentence and not as a wish, is
not yet a clear announcement of salvation for Zion (cf. e.g. Isa
40:2 "Her iniquity is pardoned"), yet it comes closer to being an
expression of hope than almost anything else in the book. It recognizes that with the fall of the city and the beginning of the exile the
flood tide of Yahweh's wrath had passed. Not so for Edom; her
judgment day was yet to come.

V
A PRAYER
(5:1–22)

1 Remember, Yahweh, what happened to us;
    Consider, and see our disgrace.
2 Our land is turned over to strangers;
    Our houses, to foreigners.
3 We have become orphans, fatherless;
    Our mothers are like widows.
4 We pay money to drink our own water,
    And must buy our own wood.
5 A yoke has been set on our neck;
    We are weary, and have no rest.
6 We made a pact with Egypt;
    And with Assyria, to get enough bread.
7 Our fathers sinned, and are no more,
    And we suffer for their iniquities.
8 Slaves have become our rulers;
    There is none to deliver us from their
        power.
9 To get bread we risk our lives
    Before the pursuer's sword.
10 Our skin is black as an oven
    From the scorch of famine.
11 They raped women in Zion;
    Virgins in the cities of Judah.
12 Their hands hanged our princes;
    They did not honor the elders.
13 They took young men to grind;
    And youths stagger from hard work.

14 The elders are gone from the gate;
    The young men no longer make music.
15 The joy of our heart is gone;
    Our dance has turned to mourning.
16 The crown has fallen from our head.
    Alas that we ever sinned!
17 At this our heart has sickened;
    These things have darkened our sight.
18 On Mount Zion, which lies desolate,
    foxes prowl about.
19 Yet you, Yahweh, rule forever;
    Your throne is eternal.
20 Why do you never think of us?
    Why abandon us so long?
21 Bring us back to you, Yahweh, and we will
      return.
    Make our days as they were before.
22 But instead you have completely rejected us;
    You have been very angry with us.

Title: *A Prayer*. Not in MT, this title is found in various Greek manuscripts; other ancient witnesses add "of Jeremiah," or "of Jeremiah the prophet."

2. *is turned over*. For this sense of *nehepkāh,* cf. Isa 60:5.

It is unnecessary to add a verb in the second colon (so tentatively BH³ *nitt*ᵉ*nū,* following Haller); as it stands the line is of a perfectly ordinary type with respect to parallelism, and though the dominant meter of the poem is 3+3, the 3+2 found here occurs also in vss. 3 and 14, though the latter are more evenly balanced in number of syllables per colon.

4. *water* and *wood* (firewood, as the plural form and the context implies), here in poetic parallelism, were evidently linked together in common speech; see Josh 9:21, 23, 27; Deut 29:10. *šātīnū,* "we drink," is perfect tense, but in this chapter the perfect is used both for past time (as probably 6, 7, 14, 15, etc.) and for present time as here and probably 5, 8, 11, 12, 13.

5. Read <*ālāh 'ōl*> *'al ṣawwārēnū,* etc. The first two words of the line have been lost through homoioarcton (that is, through having similar beginning consonants; note that Symmachus seems to preserve a greater part of the original than does MT); for a similar sequence cf. Num 19:2; I Sam 6:7. In the second colon, *nirdapnū,* "we are pursued," and *yāga'nū,* "we are weary," (omitted here) are a doublet, that is, the line existed in variant forms and both readings have been incorporated in the MT. For similar phenomena in Jeremiah, see J. Gerald Janzen, "Double Readings in the text of Jeremiah," *Harvard Theological Review* 60 (1967), 433–47. Other double readings in Lamentations may occur at 1:7; 2:9a; and 3:56. "Yoke" is a common figure for servitude; cf. 1:14; 3:27; Deut 28:48 and many other passages.

6. *We made a pact.* More literally, "gave the hand (to), shook hands with"; the translation adopted here is intended to make clear that this is not simply "stretched out the hand (in supplication)" as some render it, but "made a pact with," cf. II Kings 10:15; Ezek 17:18; Ezra 10:19; I Chron 29:24; II Chron 30:8. For a depiction of kings (Shalmaneser and Marduk-zakir-shumi) shaking hands, apparently in formal confirmation of their relation as overlord and vassal, see David Oates, "The Excavations at Nimrud (Kalhu), 1962," *Iraq* 25 (1963), Plate VII c and pp. 21–22; and cf. J. M. Munn-Rankin, "Diplomacy in Western Asia in the Early Second Millennium B.C.," *Iraq* 18 (1956), 86, for possible oblique references to such an act in the Mari texts. R. G. Boling has called to my attention a possible parallel in the Amarna letters, EA, No. 298, lines 25–29, where Yapahu of Gezer writes: "Let the king my lord know that my youngest brother is estranged from me, and has entered Muhhazu, and has given his two hands to the chief of the 'Apiru." (translation of W. F. Albright, ANET, p. 490). The reading "hands" is uncertain, but probable, and the parallel is illuminating.

7. *and . . . And.* Supplying *w,* with the Qre.

9. *pursuer's sword.* The MT has *ḥereb hammidbār,* "sword of the desert," which yields no apparent sense; commentators have taken this as a kind of kenning for "bedouin" but this is strained. Dahood's proposal, adopted here, is based on recognizing in *mdbr* the root *dbr* which occurs in the Amarna letters in the sense "drive away" and has been plausibly identified by Dahood at Ps 127:5 and II Chron 22:10; see Dahood "Hebrew-Ugaritic Lexicography, II," *Biblica* 45 (1964), 401. Compare also *Psalms III, 101–150,* fifth NOTE on Ps 127:5, with further examples. Others have proposed "heat" of the desert.

10. *is black* for *nikmārū* is based on Gr. *epeliōthē,* "has become black and blue," and the meaning "be dark" of a cognate Syriac verb. Blackening of the skin from famine is mentioned in 4:8 (cf. Job 30:30). Other ancient translations, "is shriveled," and "is heated, scorched," have been defended by modern commentators; see especially Rudolph's commentary, Albrektson ad loc., and G. R. Driver, "Notes on the Text of Lamentations," ZAW 52 (1934), 308.

11. As is normal in Hebrew poetry, the second part of this line repeats and expands what was said in the first, and one must not press the distinction between the "women" in Zion and the "virgins" in the cities of Judah as Ehrlich does with rather amusing results:

"As distinguished from *bᵉtūlōt* (virgins) *nāšīm* here means married women. Thus the enemy in general preferred virgins, but unlike the situation in the provincial towns, in Jerusalem there were also married women mixed in with them, because the wives in the capital dressed as youthfully as the young girls and so could not be distinguished from them" (*Randglossen*, VII, 53; my translation).

13. Both parts of the verse are difficult. The first part is often rendered as here, and this is perhaps correct, though the infinitive without *l* is a problem, and though *nāśā'* is not very commonly used in this sense (cf. however e.g. Jer 49:29). Another translation commonly adopted "Young men had to carry the mill" is grammatically easy, but open to the objection that a mill was not usually carried from place to place, and besides, it would not have been especially hard to have to carry an ancient hand-mill.

The Vulgate translates, "Young men were sexually abused," apparently taking Heb. *ṭḥn*, "grind," in an obscene sense. The verb is so used in Job 31:10, and scholars have pointed out a similar semantic development, from "grind" to "copulate," in other languages. In spite of the good parallel in Job, however, it is difficult to see how such a sense fits with the other half of the line.

In the second part of the verse read *bᵉ'eṣe<b>*, "from hard work," not *bā'ēṣ*, "over wood." As Ehrlich points out, the sense cannot be that youths stagger under heavy loads of wood, because *kāšal b-* means to stumble *over* something. "Youths stumble over wood" is hardly correct, so I have assumed a textual error: the *b* of original *'eṣeb* was lost from the text because of similarity to the following *k*, a kind of haplography. For *kāšal b-* followed by an abstract noun, cf. Hosea 14:1[2H]; Ps 31:10[11H]; Prov 24:16; in all these cases the *b* may be rendered "because of, from," as is done here.

16. For "crown" as a symbol of glory and honor cf. Isa 28:1, 3; Job 19:9.

17. *our heart has sickened.* Cf. 1:22 and Isa 1:5; Jer 8:18. RSV (so also Budde, Rudolph, Kraus and others) connects 17 with 19: "For this . . . for these things . . . for Mount Zion." But other examples of Heb. *'al* plus the demonstrative pronoun *zeh*, etc., at the beginning of a sentence require interpretation as referring to what precedes rather than what follows (Jer 31:26; Ps 32:6; Isa 57:6; 64:11; Jer 5:9, 29; 9:9[8H]; Amos 8:8. Jer 4:28; Micah 1:8 and Lam 1:16 are less clear). Furthermore, *'al 'ēlleh*, a plural, can

only with difficulty be taken to refer to the single condition described in vs. 18. The construction of 18 is somewhat unusual, but perhaps not totally unparalleled; the sentence-type may contain what is called a *casus pendens* in traditional Hebrew grammar. One element of the sentence, in this case a prepositional phrase '*al har ṣiyyōn,* is given prominence by being placed first; it is then referred to by a pronoun ("retrospective pronoun") later on in the clause (*bō*). For parallels with prepositional phrases, see II Sam 6:23; I Sam 9:20.

18. *foxes prowl about.* Compare the "Curse of Agade," ANET, p. 651, lines 254–55: "Over your *usga*-place, established for lustrations, May the 'fox of the ruined mounds,' glide his tail."

19. *Yet you.* The translation "Yet you" or "But you" is suggested by the use of the independent personal pronoun and the prominent position in which it is placed, whether or not one reads the conjunction *w* (not in MT, but in most of the ancient versions).

22. *But instead.* The proper translation of this verse, important for the thought of the whole poem, is disputed because of the opening words *kī 'im* (Greek and Syriac seem to omit the *'im,* but they may have simply glossed over the difficulty; in any case *kī 'im* is preferable as the more difficult reading). The following are the possibilities: (a) Sometimes in Hebrew these two words, even in combination, retain the sense each has separately: "for if . . ." and the conditional clause thus introduced is followed by a consequence: "then . . ." Thus Exod 8:21[17H] and elsewhere. This would lead to a translation here as "For if you have utterly rejected us, you have been extremely angry with us" (so Ehrlich, *Randglossen*). This is unacceptable, since the second colon does not really state the consequence of the first, but is rather a restatement of it. Note that in those cases where *kī 'im* really does mean "for if," the apodosis is usually specifically marked as such by *hinnēh* or *w*. (b) Many translate approximately as follows: "Unless you have utterly rejected us," etc., the implication being that this possibility is actually excluded. Rudolph defends this by comparing Gen 32:26 [27H] and states that this is a very common use of *kī 'im.* Yet the parallel cited, and all other cases where *kī 'im* has to be translated "unless" are only apparent, not genuine, for in these other cases it is used after a clause containing or implying a negative; the clause following *kī 'im* states a condition that must be fulfilled before the preceding statement can or should be in effect: "Not A,

unless N." Cf. Albrektson, ad loc. The logical relation of the clauses
in vss. 21 and 22 is something quite different. (c) Very similar to the
above is the translation as a question: "Or have you utterly rejected
us?" etc. This also is difficult to defend, because *kī 'im* is not elsewhere used to introduce a question. (d) The remaining possibility,
adopted here (following the Vulgate, Luther, the King James Version
and Paul Volz, *Theologische Literaturzeitung* 22 [1940], cols. 82–
83), is to translate as adversative "But you have utterly rejected
us," etc. Occasionally *kī 'im* is used as an adversative conjunction
even when there is no explicit negative in the preceding context; see
GKC, 163b.

In these cases one must understand some such statement as: "(the
foregoing is not the case), but rather. . . ." Thus II Sam 13:33
(Ktib); Num 24:22; I Sam 21:5[6H] (here one must translate
"truly, indeed"). Here in vss. 21–22, then, the sequence of thought
is, "Would that you would make things as they were; (you have not
yet done so), but rather," etc. It is too much to say that such a
rendering contradicts the statement of 20 and the prayer of 21
(so Rudolph); it simply restates the present fact: Israel does stand
under God's severe judgment. Jewish liturgical practice reflects the
understanding of vs. 22 defended here, for it is traditional not to end
public reading of this scroll with this somber verse, but to repeat
after it the prayer of vs. 21. A similar usage is followed with the
end of Isaiah, Ecclesiastes, and Malachi. For other laments which
similarly end in a low key, cf. Jer 14:9; Pss 88, 89.

COMMENT

Chapter 5 stands apart from the rest of Lamentations, especially with respect to formal features. It is not an acrostic like the other poems in the book, though it does have exactly twenty-two verses, one for each letter of the Hebrew alphabet. Metrically it is also different: it is not written in the *Qinah* (lament) meter, with unbalanced lines, but for the most part in lines whose parts balance each other. The commonest line contains three accents in each half. As compared to the rest of the book, there is in chapter 5 a much higher proportion of synonymous parallelism of a segmental type, that is, of the sort where each element in the first half-line is answered by a corresponding element in the second.

Chapter 5 is, moreover, a purer example of a recognized poetic type than any of the other poems in the book, for it follows rather closely the pattern of the "lament of the community." Probably in recognition of these differences from the other poems in the book, various Greek and Latin copies of Lamentations set chapter 5 apart as "A Prayer," "A Prayer of Jeremiah," or the like.

In ancient Israel, laments of the community were evidently composed and used in times of great national distress, when the whole nation appealed for help against its enemies. Commonly cited examples of the genre in the psalter are Pss 44; 60; 74; 79; 80; 83; and 89. Lam 5 exemplifies the salient characteristics of the type: the prayer is collective, making use of "we," the first-person plural pronoun; it contains a description of the distress; and there is an appeal to God for help. Lam 5 is remarkable, however, for the relatively short appeal for help and the correspondingly long description of the nation's trouble; in this respect it is closer to the other chapters of Lamentations.

Outline

A. The present troubles and their cause, vss. 1–18
   1. A call for God to notice, 1.
   2. The troubles and their cause, 2–18.
B. Praise of God and an appeal for help, vss. 19–21.
C. Closing lament, vs. 22.

The first verse, with its "Remember . . . consider, and see" is not yet an explicit call for help, but only a preliminary: God should take notice of their distress. This distress is at once characterized as "disgrace." Ancient Israelites possessed a keen sense of honor and of the proper order of things, so that when trouble came they would complain as often and as bitterly of the shame as of the physical loss or pain, as Claus Westermann (in "Struktur und Geschichte der Klage im Alten Testament," ZAW 66 [1954], 54) points out, comparing e.g. Pss 79:4; 89:41, 50[42, 51H]; 123:3, 4.

In vs. 2 the translation "our land" has been chosen in an attempt to reflect approximately the range of meaning of Heb. *naḥᵃlātēnū,* which may refer either to personal estates, held as a grant from God (Josh 24:28), or to the land as a whole, "the good land which Yahweh your God gave you as a possession (*naḥᵃlāh*)," Deut 4:21, a favorite idea especially in Deuteronomy. Here the parallel with "houses" (cf. Micah 2:2) suggests but does not necessitate the former interpretation. In any case, the first complaint is that an order which God himself established has been overturned; both lands and houses ought to have been the inalienable gift of God (I Kings 21:3), and they are now held by strangers. Note the sequence "land . . . houses . . . water" (vss. 2–4); Deut 6:10–11 has the same order.

"Orphans" and "widows" (vs. 3) were recognized in the ancient Near East as the classes most defenseless against aggression, and this pair is linked in poetry already in very early biblical texts (e.g. Ps 68:5) and earlier still in Ugaritic poetry. Thus this line should not be made into an explicit reference to the slaughter and deportation of males; the sense is: "all of us (males included) have become defenseless."

Like "land" in vs. 2, so the "rest" of vs. 5 points to more

than a physical loss. As especially von Rad has pointed out, in *The Problem of the Hexateuch and Other Essays,* pp. 94–102, an important Old Testament theological theme is that God gives his elect people *rest* in the promised land, especially rest from their enemies (e.g. Deut 12:10; 25:19; II Sam 7:1, 11). "We have no rest" means not only "we are very weary," but "one sign of our status as God's people has been removed."

A reflection on the cause of this distress now interrupts the depiction of troubles. Verses 6 and 7 evidently refer to the past rather than to the present, for in the years just after the Babylonian conquest it is difficult to imagine that there could have been any trafficking with Egypt. (Thus also *'aššūr* here is to be taken literally, as a reference to Assyria, not as a title for Babylon. Egypt and Assyria are often linked as a poetic pair even where one or the other is not especially appropriate; Egypt is mentioned first eleven out of fourteen times.) This is a reference to the policy of making foreign alliances, favored by many of the kings and typically denounced by the prophets; cf. esp. Jer 2:18, 36; Hosea 7:11; 12:1[2H]. These alliances were attractive to Judah not only for strategic reasons but also for economic considerations. It may not be pressing too far to see in the phrase "to get enough bread" a link to a complex of Old Testament imagery: Israel, the wife of Yahweh, has been unfaithful with "lovers," that is, other gods and nations, and falsely believes these lovers are the ones who "give me my bread and my water, my wool and my flax, my oil and my drink" (Hosea 2:5[7H]; cf. 1:2 above).

The writer of Lamentations labels these alliances sin (vs. 7) and confesses his own generation's share in the guilt of the fathers. This verse has a superficial resemblance to the cynical popular saying quoted in Jer 31:29 and Ezek 18:2: "The fathers have eaten sour grapes; and the children's teeth are set on edge," but the tone and intention is much different here: the writer does not dissociate himself from the fathers—they are *"our* fathers"—or from their sin. Compare vs. 16: "We have sinned!" The verse expresses his understanding of, and acquiescence in, the judgment foretold in the terms of their covenant with God; the sins of the fathers are now being visited on their children (Exod 20:5). Jeremiah says much the same thing, in one verse, as what Lam 5 says in vss. 7 and 16: "We have sinned against Yahweh from our youth, we and our fathers" (Jer 3:25).

Then, at vs. 8, the description of the nation's distress is resumed. The "slaves" who rule are the Babylonian officials (cf. II Kings 25:24), especially, one may surmise, the lower officials with whom the people actually came in contact, and who were especially insolent and brutal. The verse recalls Prov 30:21–22, which lists as one of four unbearable things "a slave when he comes to rule"; compare also Isa 3:4, 12; Eccles 10:16.

Since the text refers to the lack of law and order in the land (vs. 9), to continued famine (vs. 10), and to atrocities (vss. 11–12), it seems that the poem was written in the days just after the fall of the city, when conditions were still especially unsettled. The reference to Judaean "princes" (vs. 12) is not necessarily out of harmony with II Kings 25:12, which says that only the poorest of the land were left behind, for this general statement (if it is not simply poetic license) does not exclude the possibility that nobles who somehow escaped the first roundup of prisoners were later caught and executed. If it is correct to see a reference to grinding in vs. 13, note that grinding was a shameful occupation for a young man, work for women of the lower classes (Isa 47: 2) or for prisoners (Samson, Judg 16:21).

Verse 18 is not only the end of this section, but also its climax. Mount Zion is the central symbol of God's presence, the visible sign of Israel's election—and it is a deserted ruin. At one level, the statement that foxes prowl there expresses the idea that the holy temple site is profaned by the presence of wild animals. At another level, this is a way of saying that an ancient curse had been carried out, just as the prophets had predicted. One of the curses traditionally associated with the covenant, as with ancient treaties, was that wild animals should make their home in the ruined city of any faithless treaty partner. The ruin and profanation of Zion, then, is a sign that this is God's own action, his punishment for breach of covenant. For biblical parallels, see e.g. Isa 13:19–22; 34:11–17; Zeph 2:13–15. For a fuller discussion, see Hillers, *Treaty-Curses*, pp. 44–54.

The little hymn-like verse which follows (vs. 19) prepares the way for the prayer that is expressed in vs. 20. This acknowledgment of God's eternal dominion has counterparts in other communal laments (Pss 44:1–8[2–9H]; 74:12–17; 80:1–2; 89:1–18 [2–19H]); even in the deepest trouble Israel did not forget to hymn God's praises. (The question "Why?" is a common one in national laments; see the discussion and list of occurrences in Westermann, ZAW 66 [1954], 44–80.) The idea of God's unchanging sovereign might is extended in the prayer (vs. 21), to include an acknowledgment of his power also over the springs of human action, and over human fortunes. "Bring us back" might mean either "change our fortunes" or "help us repent"; in this passage, with its "to you" (see NOTE), the latter is intended. This is a prayer for repentance, much like "Create and make in us new and contrite hearts." One may compare Jer 31:18, which is nearly identical in its wording: "Bring me back that I may return." The idea of national restoration comes only in the second half of the verse.

As the poet writes, however, there is not yet any sign of favorable action by God, and the poem and book end, not in despair, yet very soberly.

INDEX OF AUTHORS

INDEX OF BIBLICAL PASSAGES